SPOKES

The Process That Creates Success in All Areas of Life

JOE DEARING

Praise for *SPOKES*

I have read Joe's book and I must say it is very inspirational! I feel that sharing your past will help people see by using the techniques provided that they can reach their goals and how to go about it.

I also had struggles and mistakes from decisions in my earlier years along with a troubled home environment. Over the years, I have tried to work hard at bettering myself in many ways. Some of my education was through the school of hard knocks. After reading Joe's book, I will definitely use the Spoke method to improve the areas in which I am lacking. I want to have a well-rounded wheel and my spokes aligned.

I see the potential for Joe's *Spokes* to be used to help others personally and professionally such as in recovery programs through churches or other associations, youth programs to assist teens, young adults struggling to figure out life after living at home, and the list goes on.

Susan Ott,
20/20 Imaging Sales Manager

❀

Spokes is straight from the heart, written in a way that anyone can relate to. It shows us all that our past does not equal our future. Joe inspires us to overcome our personal obstacles with a sensible and workable approach. *Spokes* is great reading for all those that want a more fulfilling life. I highly recommend it.

Mark Foley,
Sandler Sales

❀

In '*Spokes, The Process That Creates Success in All Areas of Life,*' Joe masterfully dismantles the chains of the past, illuminating a path towards a future of limitless potential. Through his transparency, he shares heartfelt stories and empowering wisdom, this book resonates as a beacon of hope, reminding us that our history doesn't define us - it's the choices we make now that propel us toward the Purpose-Filled Life we were created to live. '*Spokes*' is a compelling testament to the resilience of the human spirit and a guidebook for rewriting our own narratives. A must-read for anyone seeking to Align their Dreams, Chart their Course and Navigate themselves to the Purpose-Filled Life they were created to Live!!!

M. Kevin Davis,
Author, International Speaker, Executive Coach and Podcast Host

❀

This remarkable memoir chronicles the transformative journey of an individual who triumphed over adversity by setting and achieving extraordinary goals. Through his experiences, the author imparts invaluable wisdom and motivation, making this book a true source of inspiration for anyone seeking personal growth and fulfillment.

One of the most compelling aspects of this book is its emphasis on the importance of setting goals. The author shares his own experiences of setting ambitious objectives and working tirelessly towards them, demonstrating that with dedication and perseverance, anything is possible. The book provides a step-by-step guide to goal setting, offering practical tools and strategies that can be applied to real-life situations.

Whether you're a student seeking clarity in your educational journey or a professional striving for career advancement, *"Spokes"* offers invaluable insights and practical advice that can be applied to any goal-setting endeavor.

"Spokes" is a compelling life story book that has the power to transform lives. It beautifully illustrates the importance of setting goals, while also providing readers with the tools and motivation necessary to turn dreams into reality. Through the author's personal anecdotes and timeless wisdom, this book serves as a guiding light, encouraging readers to embrace their passions, overcome obstacles, and create a life of purpose and fulfillment. I wholeheartedly recommend it to anyone seeking personal and professional growth.

Charles Bagley,
Retired Business Executive

✿

Being the age of 23 I have been more interested in books that give a guide to the way one may live their life. I had the opportunity to read the book Joe Dearing has written, *Spokes*. Joe takes the time to give his story and the book is written in his perspective of how he's pivoted his life. I am blessed and humbled because it brings me back to life. I would recommend this book because it shows a young man turns into his authentic self without questioning. Thank you, Joe!

Ashley Chandler,
EMT at Acadian Ambulance

✿

CONTENTS

FOREWORD

THE WRONG DIRECTIONS

Are you where you want to be in life?

Does life happen to you, or do you happen to life?

Were you given the wrong directions, or no direction at all?

In the fledgling stage of Zig Ziglar's speaking career he accepted a free speech over two hours from his home by car. He wanted to arrive two hours early so he could get a feel for the room and meet the hosts. HIs dream was to become a motivational speaker and he knew he had a lot of work to do. He set out early that day to pursue his dream.

When he got to the outskirts of the city he realized he needed directions to the place where he was speaking, so he stopped at a roadside full-service gas station, common back in the early 1960s. The helpful gas station attendant gave him step-by-step instructions on how to find the address he was looking for and he wrote them down in detail and verified them with the attendant. He got back on the road again, excited about what was to come.

Lost.

Forty-five minutes later, after following the directions step by step, Zig Ziglar knew something was wrong and he was lost. A sign confirmed he was 30 miles further away from his destination than he was when he stopped to ask for directions!

Respond or react? The choice is yours.

What if Zig Ziglar had reacted? What if the voice in his head had said, "Oh, no! My reputation as a speaker is ruined even before my career has started! There is no way I will make it on time, so I might as well just go home and give up on this crazy dream."

But Zig Ziglar didn't react, he responded. He chose to stop and ask for directions again, and this time he was given the right directions. He got there on time and the rest is history - over 250 million people impacted by his speeches and books.

It's not your fault, but it is your responsibility.

Zig Ziglar understood that it was not his fault he was given bad directions, but it was his responsibility, once he realized the directions were bad, to go out and seek the right directions.

Are you where you want to be in life? Are you experiencing balanced success in every area of life? I have good news for you. Where you are in life is likely not all your fault. Well-meaning people often give bad directions, or no direction at all. If you are like most people, you have also compounded the situation with some bad choices - like going down the wrong curvy road at 100 mph!

"You are what you are and where you are because of what has gone into your mind. You can change what you are and where you are by changing what goes into your mind." Zig Ziglar

Spokes is a life-changing book that shows you how you can create the life you have always wanted. The combination of not blaming yourself for the bad directions you were given, and then taking 100% ownership of your choices and current situation, empowers you to choose to find the right directions and take action.

Joe Dearing wrote *Spokes* with love in his heart for every person like him. His personal examples and experiences give you hope, no matter where you are on the road of life. Joe's step-by-step examples of what you can do are powerful and his stories are inspiring. Have your pen handy as you take notes and journal your thoughts throughout the book. I am proud and grateful to call Joe a good friend, and I know he will bless you as he has blessed me.

Choose To Win!
Tom Ziglar - CEO of Zig Ziglar Corporation

INTRODUCTION

H i everyone, my name is Joe. Not your average Joe. I am a Ziglar Legacy Certified Trainer, and I have been a student of Zig Ziglar for most of my adult life. I was fortunate enough to work for the Ziglar Corporation while Zig was at his peak. He taught me so much, and now I want to carry his legacy forward. I want to share with you my story of how I was able to overcome many challenges and shortcomings through a process of setting and achieving goals. Here is my story and how I was able to use these principles, along with the love of God, to transform myself.

First, I want to talk a little bit about the physiological changes our bodies go through when they are subjected to harsh conditions. Think about your soft hands. When introduced to an axe, your soft hands hang on tight and are subjected to continuous harsh conditions. Banging over and over, they will first begin to hurt. As the harsh conditions continue, they begin to blister. The blisters then pop, causing excruciating pain. Keep on subjecting them to those conditions over time and they will begin to develop a hard outer layer of skin to protect the soft inside. Your hands become hard, rough, and calloused.

Life can be the same way. When we are subjected to hard times and hard circumstances, the heart can become calloused and hard. We build walls so that nothing gets in because we are protecting ourselves from getting hurt. You know what the difference is between your hands getting calloused and your heart getting calloused? Getting a hardened heart is a choice, and you can choose another path. A path that isn't easy but is worth it. You really must learn to forgive yourself and others if you expect to reach your potential.

My mentor Zig Ziglar used to tell a story about Spindletop, and I would like to share it with you. At the turn of the twentieth century in Beaumont, Texas, oil was discovered. The owner of the property was told that if the potential oil well was as productive as predicted, he would become very wealthy. In those days the derricks were made from wood, and the productivity of the oil well was determined by the amount of damage caused to the derricks. In this case, when the oil began to gush, the derrick was obliterated. This was the world's introduction to Spindletop, the most productive oil well in history. Three major oil companies are said to have been formed from that one single well. The property owner became an instant millionaire, or did he?

The fact is, he became a millionaire when he acquired the property. But until they drilled for oil and brought it to the surface, then took it to the marketplace, it was worthless. Here's my point: our potential lies deep inside us. Until we dig deep and tap into our potential, then bring it to the surface and use it in the marketplace, we cannot imagine the possibilities that exist for us.

How do we do that? How do we tap into the "Spindletop" that lies deep within us? I will share that information with you in this book.

The reason I am telling my story is because I want you to know that if some poor, high school drop out with a drug addiction, who filed for bankruptcy and ended up divorced because of the poor decisions he made can figure this success thing out, so can you.

If you can change the way you see yourself, give it your all, create your roadmap to success, and follow it to the letter, you will be able to accomplish great new things in no time. True success is when you have balance in all areas of life, not just the money. My friend Tom Ziglar says it this way, "The fastest way to success is to replace bad habits with good ones."

I decided to write this book because I was able to implement a strategy that allowed me to grow and have success in all areas of life. As you read, you will find out:

- I was a failure in school, and I dropped out because I was a drug addict.
- I was a failure in marriage and got divorced because I was an adulterer.
- I was a failure in business and filed for bankruptcy because I couldn't manage money.
- I was a failure in my spiritual walk because I abandoned God and tried to do things my own way.
- I was a failure physically because the stress left me massively overweight, struggling with depression, and not knowing how to deal with the things life was throwing at me.

I met a man named Zig Ziglar whose "wheel of life" goal-setting strategy changed me in all those areas. This book is not only a comeback story but, rather, a strategic plan that can help others who are struggling in any area of life. My objective with this book is to help people understand that failure is an event, not a person. You can change anything you want; as long as you create a roadmap for yourself to follow, you can get to where you want to be.

SCHOOL DAZE

I began life as a little boy with a gentle heart and a pure mind. My mother was a young woman of 18 when she got pregnant with me. She grew up in southern California and lived in Simi Valley with her four siblings. She was gorgeous. I remember an old black and white photo we had of her. I thought she was so beautiful. She was sweet, tenderhearted, and loving—that's how I thought of her when I was a little boy.

She married my dad who also had come from a pretty big family; he had five siblings. They were all his half-siblings because his biological father died in a tragic car accident when my dad was only three years old. Dad was the oldest of the kids, and he had to take care of them because his mom and stepdad were heavy drinkers. Funny thing to mention, my dad's name is Dearing and my mom's maiden name was Deering. I was literally one letter away from having some serious birth defects.

When I was born in 1967, Los Angeles was going through a transformation. The hippy culture was the new trend, and my mom and dad were right in the mix. It was a crazy time for sure. Dad rode a Harley, and he was a true old-school biker. He was a member of the Free Wheelers Motorcycle Club. He was in and out of jail for different things—nothing too major—but he was definitely a crazy dude who hung out with crazy people, and he was always having a good time. Before I was born, he was in a massive car accident and broke almost every bone in his body. He was tough, and he was mean.

My father made a living fixing cars. He was one of the best mechanics around, so getting work was easy for him. However, due to his lifestyle, he bounced around. I remember moving a lot. I was born in Glendale, California; then we moved to Van Nuys, Burbank, Camarillo, Simi Valley, Thousand Oaks; Las Vegas, Nevada; Chandler, Arizona; Portland, Oregon; Springfield, Missouri; and Arlington, Texas. I probably left out four or five places, but this was all before I was even 13 years old. Dad's nickname was "the Gypsy."

My mom and dad got married and divorced a couple of times during my childhood because of his destructive behavior. Despite that, he really was a fun guy who loved the adrenalin rush that came from four wheeling in his Toyota Land Cruiser and various jeeps over the years. We would climb the mountains and run down the riverbeds of Lake Piru and Fillmore, California. We would have water coming in the doors of his lifted jeep as we drove down the river. A couple of times we rolled that jeep. Once we were going up a big steep hill, and a shock blew out. We rolled it all the way to the bottom of the hill but still managed to get it upright and drive it home.

We would often load up the jeep, the sand rail dune buggy, and dirt bikes and head to the sand dunes of Pismo Beach. Pismo was a place where the sand dunes spread for miles and miles off the central California coast. Hundreds if not thousands of crazy people would go out there to have fun on dirt bikes, sand rails, jeeps, four wheelers and dune buggies. Everyone loved climbing the pristine sand dunes and ripping their machines as fast as they would go up, down, and even around those beautiful dunes. A lot of fun which often was accompanied by a lot of pain. One day I was helping my dad put the trailer on the ball hitch. I was guiding him back and grabbed the hitch to move it over to meet the ball; as I did, the trailer fell onto the ball with my finger inside the hitch. There was blood everywhere. My middle finger was almost completely severed, but doctors were able to stitch it back on. That was just one of many weird tragedies that happened back then.

I remember being in the backseat of the jeep one night as my dad flew it through the sand at about 60 mph. We were racing another guy down the sand highway at Pismo Beach, and we hit a three-foot drop. A friend of my dad's was riding shotgun and must not have had his shoulder harness on because he ate the dash and completely lost his nose. I got out of the jeep, and there was a puddle of blood in the sand (it is hard to make a puddle in sand, so he was clearly losing a ton of blood). My dad grabbed the dude by the face and tried to form a nose back on his face from his cheeks. The bleeding slowed, and we got him to a hospital. The guy survived, and everything worked out, but his nose made a serious left turn after that.

Those days were fun for me as I also had a need for speed and loved the crazy antics of my dad's lead foot and his fearlessness in driving up massive mountains and sand dunes. A Toyota he built could do wheelies. We were at an intersection one day, and my dad said, "Check this out." The light turned green, and he slammed this B&M quick click shifter into gear, and we launched. It stood straight up, and all this little kid could do was hang on. He was an adrenaline junky and loved the thrill that came along with off-roading.

My dad bought me my first motorcycle when I was about five years old. It was just a little minibike, but I rode that thing in our back yard every day. After that, he got me a go-cart, then an XR75 dirt bike. I rode the wheels off anything he built for me. One day my mom bought me my first real full-size dirt bike. It was a 1978 RM 125 with the full floater suspension: the first mono-shock suspension on a dirt bike. One reason I call this book *Spokes* is because I grew up on two wheels and always rode or raced motorcycles growing up. My dad took me out to the Indian Dunes to ride and race this four wheel "Honda Odyssey" when I was young. The thrill of racing made me want to ride as much as I possibly could. Every day I was riding my dirt bike in the backyard. I probably really irritated our neighbors but I was hooked.

I was a pretty good rider, so when I was 12 years old, I took a job delivering newspapers. It was cool because, at the time, we lived in Thousand Oaks, California, and I had this Honda XR75. So, I got up at like 5 a.m. and would fold or roll the huge stack of papers that were delivered to my house each day. Then I would sling this large bag over my head that carried about 50 newspapers in the front and 50 in the back. I got on my mini bike and delivered the newspapers in our neighborhood before going to school. Each month I would go door to door to collect the money from my newspaper customers. That's what I was doing at 12 years old, and it was one of the best times of my life.

On February 2, 1979, in Thousand Oaks California, my mom gave birth to my little sister. I was 12 and remember having to care for the baby over the summer. I taught her how to eat food and pee in the toilet because I was her big brother babysitter that summer. My dad owned a shop called B&G Automotive on Thousand Oaks Blvd (that real estate is worth millions now, crazy). Business was good, but dad had an alcohol and substance abuse problem (he loved cocaine), so we sold the shop and moved to Springfield, Missouri. I went to Kickapoo Junior High School for a few months, and my extremely cool, Super Goose BMX bike that my granddad bought me was stolen from the quarter arcade where I was playing one day. I was ready to "Kickapoo" after that. We were there for only six months, and we moved to Arlington, Texas. Constantly moving meant starting over at new schools. It made me a better communicator, I think, but I never really felt like I was at home.

During the few months we lived in Arlington, my parents decided to divorce. My mom divorced him because he was a physically and verbally abusive alcoholic. Dad would get violent and beat my mother and me from time to time after a drinking binge. I found him passed out on the front lawn one day when I left to walk to school. He was an awesome dude when he wasn't drunk. The problem was, he was drunk almost every day. My mom stayed in Texas with my little sister who was only maybe one year old at the time. I missed my friends, so I decided to move with my dad back to California. But as it turned out, moving back probably wasn't the best idea. Dad got into selling weed and coke, and I was getting into his stash quite often.

I want you to know that, today, my dad is an amazing guy with a brilliant sense of humor and a wealth of knowledge—I often go to him for advice. But he struggled with alcoholism and drug addiction until he finally showed up one day 37 years ago, and said, "I'm done." He went to an inpatient program at Schick Hospital and was rehabilitated in a few weeks. We'll come back to this later.

We always went off-roading with my uncle, David. This uncle was an all-around awesome man. His son, Dave, was my age, and we were thicker than thieves growing up. Dave was like a brother to me my entire childhood. He always picked on me, but I was pretty tough. I played football with him; he was a really good all-around athlete.

"Silver Spoons" was little Dave's handle on the CB radio when we were out four-wheeling together. He was good looking and could always pick up the chicks with his charming and funny personality. Once, we went to an all-night dance down in the San Fernando Valley, and four guys started pushing me around. Dave grabbed one of the dudes and knocked him out, then pummeled the second guy. The other two decided to leave me alone at that point. Earlier that day, Dave and I had gone to Miller's Outpost in Simi Valley, and he picked up the coolest shirt. It was a nice pastel button up with kind of new-wave vibe. But by the time he finished with the two guys at the party, that new shirt was ripped to shreds. When we got back to his house, he stapled it to the wall in his bedroom. My cousin Dave recently passed away from cancer, and I was with him in his final moments. I miss him dearly.

There always seemed to be some traumatic event taking place. Once, when I was seven, I fell while riding my skateboard. When I hit the ground, I was knocked out; David got help. It was a guy in a Cadillac who stopped and put me in the back of his car and took me to the hospital. At the hospital, doctors took x-rays of my head and thought they saw a tumor growing on my brain. They operated, but there was no tumor, so they sent me home.

When I was nine, I had so many problems with ear infections that I ended up having a radical mastoidectomy surgery on my right ear. The procedure left me almost completely deaf in my right ear because they removed my ear drum and supporting bone structure that connected my inner ear. I still to this day can barely hear out of my right ear. It was during those days that I spent a lot of time with my Uncle David.

My Uncle David was a very tough guy—a football coach—but he always showed me a little more grace than the other guys because he knew what I was going through at home. I lived with Uncle David for a while growing up to avoid the toxic atmosphere in our house. Dad was always yelling at my mom and throwing anything he could get his hands on—chairs, lamps, glassware. One time, he hit me in the face with a full can of beer because I lost my house key. Times were tough in my house, so I was happy for the opportunity to hang out with Uncle David.

He taught me some pretty cool stuff; he even coached me in Pop Warner football for a season, but I was simply too small to be competitive. He tried me at wide receiver, but I was too slow. Then I played the safety position, but always seemed to get burned, allowing the other team to score. Eventually, he found the perfect position for me—on the bench. It was perfect, and it didn't matter because I don't remember ever seeing my dad at any of my games. Mom was there and was pissed because Uncle David benched me, but honestly, my favorite position in any sport was "left out."

It was around that time that I started smoking weed with my Uncle Bud (ironically enough). I was around 11 years old, and the 18-year-old, super cool Uncle Bud was living with us at the time. I remember him taking me to Van Nuys where his buddy was a dope dealer to get some Thai Stick. It was some "killer weed," he said, that was from Thailand, and it was tied to a stick. After leaving the dealer's house, we went to a different aunt and uncle's house to smoke the weed with them. Here I am 11 years old, hanging out with my aunt and uncles, smoking Thai Stick, and feeling like I was so cool. It was the beginning of a childhood filled with drug addiction, pain, and disappointment.

I don't blame anyone in my past for my failures; I own all my mistakes. I did the same thing to my little sister years later when she was about 13. I thought I was being cool—getting her high when she was young. The truth is, I am partially to blame for leading a lot of people in the wrong direction. That's why I feel convicted now to try to help as many people as I can. But here is the truth: as we get older, the stupid decisions we make can no longer be blamed on anything or anyone but ourselves. We must forgive people, not only those who may have done us wrong, but we should also forgive ourselves. Then we can use what was intended for bad, in a good way to help others. This is one of the first things to do if you really want to turn your life around: own your mistakes and forgive others.

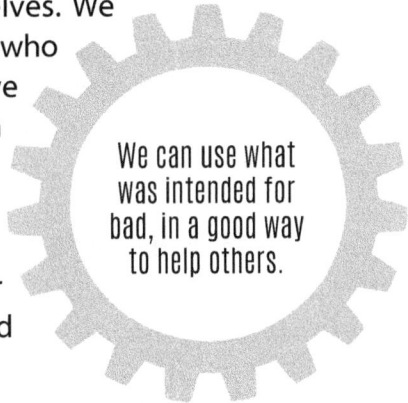

> We can use what was intended for bad, in a good way to help others.

Anyway, I was very small for my age and had large "buck" teeth, so I got picked on all the time at school. Kids called me "Bucky Beaver" and said, "You can eat corn on the cob through a picket fence." I was punched and thumped many times. One of the "thumpings" I got on a regular basis was the "luper." It was a thing this one kid always did to me. He would relax his ring finger and thump me on the head like a whip with his fingernail. The dreaded luper... Later in life I would "luper" my kids on the head, so I was able to get some payback at their expense.

I definitely had no self-esteem, and I really wasn't very good at any sports, so I gravitated towards the outcasts of the school. When you are always the "new kid" at school, you are an outcast. So whenever I arrived at a new school, I would always just go to the back parking lot or wherever the smokers would hang out. I would show up with a joint in my mouth and introduce myself, "How's it going? I'm Stoner Joe." I would always come away from those awkward first days at a new school with a handful of new pothead friends.

I hated Texas because, when I showed up in 1980 wearing parachute pants and checkered Vans tennis shoes, they didn't know what to think of me. I remember this redneck kid always waiting to pick on me after school. I fought that dude almost every day. One day he spit his Copenhagen in my eyes and punched me in the face. Needless to say, when my dad said, "I'm going back to Cali, you want to go with me?" I was all over it.

I moved with Dad to Quartz Hill, then Thousand Oaks again. He was never around when he was living the single life, so I moved back to Irving, Texas, to live with my mom. I went back and forth between Texas and California, never really finding a place I could call home.

I gravitated towards the "freaks" as most of them listened to the same hard rock, heavy metal music and had the same type of attitude I did. We hated school, always skipped, and always got high. I was rebellious too, I guess I felt like I had a reason to demolish your mailbox or dump water into your gas tank. In December, I would go out at night and literally pull the Christmas lights off houses and throw the bulbs at passing cars. I went through a phase where I stole gas caps just to be destructive and piss people off.

I never studied in school, never did homework, and never paid attention in class. I mastered the art of forging a note and would always be missing school and forging notes to get excused for being absent. When I actually did go to school, I usually ended up in some chaos or trouble. I remember a few times I did some very bad things in school. One day I decided to take a hit of LSD during class. I was flicking matches into a trash can so I could watch the tracers coming off the match. I ended up accidentally starting a fire in one of the trash cans in the lunchroom. The entire cafeteria filled with smoke as I walked out laughing. The janitor put another trash can inside the one I set on fire and quickly extinguished the flames. I got expelled for that stunt.

Another time, I got busted because I was rolling a joint when a teacher came around the corner. I got caught red-handed with a bag of weed in my lap. That put me in alternative school. I actually loved the alternative school because a bus would pick me up, and I didn't have to walk. I would sit in the back seat, open the window, and smoke pot on the way to school every day. The entire alternative school population was dopers, for the most part, so I had a bunch of friends there.

When I lived with my mom in Irving, she qualified for Section 8 housing, so we lived in the Raible Place Apartments. One night, I snuck out and hotwired my mom's VW bug. My buddy Scott and I were driving in reverse (like idiots), and I ran right into Scott's car. I completely trashed the entire rear end of my mom's Bug (where the engine is). That wasn't the only time. One night after Mom went to bed, I stole her keys and took her nicer car out to party with some friends. I ended up in a ditch. The cops picked me up and took me to the police station where my mom had to come get me. I was always in trouble, and I never really cared.

The Raible Place Apartments were actually very nice and well kept. Although it was Section 8 housing, it was the 80's and residents were required to work in order to get benefits. My mom worked very hard but was only paid around $5 an hour. That is how she qualified to get us into a very cool three-bedroom place. Even though we paid a lower rate for our apartment, Mom was a single parent supporting two kids, so we were broke all the time. But I look back and feel blessed for that time. Some great friends came out of that place.

My first job in Irving was at Taco Bell. I was only 15 years old but was taking a class in school called CVAE COOP, a vocational program which gave class credit for working. My mom really needed the help, so I started working the drive-thru window. My manager approached me about a scheme to embezzle money from the drive-thru. Long story short, I pick up on stuff quick and soon was making some easy money. The boss split it with me, and then he would usually give me his half of the money for a bag of weed. Which I always had on hand.

I was always fighting with my mom. I would say disrespectful things to her. One day she came home, and I was in my bedroom getting high with the stereo blasting. (I had the most amazing stereo system. Two, 400-watt amplifiers powered the two Peavy SP3 speakers. That all ran through my Fisher stereo system from the mixing board. I had a full-blown concert sound system in my bedroom when I was 15.) I would point my speakers out the window and jam the entire "quad," the middle of the apartment complex, where there was a big grass field and a basketball court. All the kids from the apartments would be playing there after school, and I would jam Motley Crue out the window as loud as it would go. I had a microphone and would turn up the reverb and then speak in my deepest voice, "THIS IS GOD!" Everyone would be looking around trying to figure out where the voice was coming from. Great times.

I had a pot plant growing in my closet. There was also a lawn chair in the closet and two speakers mounted on the wall. I would just sit in there and get high listening to Pink Floyd or Led Zepplin. The room was covered in hard rock magazine pictures torn from the Hit Parader and Circus magazines I collected. The ceiling was covered in tapestries of various rock artists like Rush, Motley Crue, Ozzy—you name—it if it was rock, it was on the wall or the ceiling leaving no wall space at all for anything else.

Anyway, when I say my stereo was cranked, I mean it. The apartment building was shaking, and the police were outside often, telling me to turn it down. One day, Mom had had enough. She opened the door and scratched my album while trying to turn it off. I responded to that with, "Don't be lame." That was the last straw. She screamed, "Don't you call me lame! I will show you lame!" and started smacking me upside the head. Soon after, she sent me and my sister back to Cali to live with our dad for the summer.

At this time, my dad was living with his new girlfriend in Newbury Park. I went to hang with them, and it wasn't long before I was in some serious trouble. Dad had me working on a Jaguar E Type. Its long nose was sleek, and its huge 12-cylinder engine was a remarkable machine. I was supposed to pull the water pump off the car for Dad. To do that, nearly the entire front end of the car had to come off. (I can tell you this, looking back, I learned a lot of stuff working on these cars with my dad. I could rebuild a motor by the time I was 13. The relationship with him was weird, he has no idea even to this day how much he influenced me—both good and bad.)

After a couple of long days working on the car, I was able to get away. I jumped on my BMX bike and started riding into Thousand Oaks to meet my buddy Jeff. On the way, I took a little smoke break and fired up a big doobie. I got high and then took off on my bike again towards the Oaks Mall where I was to meet Jeff. I never made it because, when I wasn't paying attention, I ran out in front of a jeep full of surfers on their way to the beach, and they ran me over. I was tossed about 120 feet down the hill and found myself barely able to breath.

I was rushed to the hospital where I had a ruptured spleen and internal bleeding. I was taken into surgery right away and somehow managed to survive, but that stunt sent me right back to Mom's house in Texas. This time, things were different. The movie *Fast Times at Ridgemont High* was out, and the character of Jeff Spicoli was me in real life. Long hair, surfer slang, and a So-Cal dialect that tortured the English language. This time, I was an instant hit in Texas, and everyone loved me. "Stoner Joe" was now the coolest dude on campus, but the problems only got worse for me.

I worked to try to help my mom, and the Winn Dixie was paying pretty good for a stocking position, so I took it. It was there that I met a few guys who had their own apartment down the street. They were looking to score some drugs, so I started selling them anything they wanted. With a name like Stoner Joe and the reputation I had, trust me, I was well connected and had the entrepreneurial spirit necessary to be a good drug dealer. I spent about a year and a half there before Mom and I had another episode that got me kicked out. It was bad. One night as I was asleep, she climbed on top of me and started hitting me. (I don't really remember why, but I'm sure I did something really stupid and deserved it.) Naturally I woke up confused. When I shoved her off me, she hit her head on the wall. I immediately was put on an airplane and never came back to Raible Place after that.

I ended up back in California once again, only now my dad lived in Paso Robles. I had only lived there a few months when my dad approached me one day and said, "Joe, I'm sorry, but I must make some changes. I've decided to go to rehab. I will be back in a few weeks."

By that time, I was 17 years old, and I was failing every class. I was smoking cocaine, weed—and sometimes, meth—daily. I'm not saying this to place blame on my dad but growing up with drugs in the house didn't help much. I started smoking weed when I was around 11 years old and by 17, I was a total drug addict. In life we are often given the wrong directions so we end up lost. I believe this was the case with my dad. He decided one day to get good directions and it changed his life.

> In life we are often given the wrong directions so we end up lost.

After a short stay in rehab, Dad returned home with a message for me. He said, "I know you are always high, and I can't be around that anymore. You need to move out."

I called my mom, but she was not going to deal with my antics anymore, so I did what I thought was best, I dropped out of high school and started selling drugs for a living. I lived on the streets for a couple of months. There was an old, abandoned RV trailer that I moved into for a few weeks. My dad had a towing company and an impound lot that this trailer was parked on in the very far back corner. I would go to his house during the daytime while he was at the shop working, and I would steal food and take it back to the trailer at night. This began to get old quickly, so one day I decided it was time to do something. I drove down to San Louis Obispo to talk to an Army recruiter. About the time I got there, my car started to overheat. I popped the hood, and it was a blown head gasket. I walked into the recruiter's office shaking my head.

He said, "What are you wanting to do?" I said I wanted to get as far away from here as possible. He said, "Four years and you can go to Germany."

I said, "Let's do it." Well, it wasn't that easy because I was only 17 and did not have my diploma. He said, "I'm going to need a parent's signature." I explained to him that my car was toast, and I would need a ride up to Paso for that signature. So, two uniformed service members drove me to my dad's auto shop in a green Army-looking sedan.

When the three of us arrived at the shop, I could see disappointment in my dad's eyes. As we approached, he said, "What the hell have you done this time?"

I told him, "I joined the Army; just sign this paper, and you'll never see me again." He signed it, and I asked him to go pick up my car and give it to Mr. Adams, the man who lived across the street. He was a very poor black guy, an old veteran, he would come to the shop on those late nights where I would be up there fixing my car, and I figured he needed the car more than I did.

I could see my dad watching as we pulled away from the shop. He actually looked like he was proud of me for the first time in my life.

I want to pause my story for a moment right here because I want to talk about the importance of family. Maybe you relate to the dad in my story and need help with an addiction issue. Maybe you are the mom who is in a hard situation, financially strapped and trying to figure out how to handle a kid who is running you ragged. Or maybe you are the guy who is just lost and needs to find his way.

This book is going to help you regardless of who or where you are in the spectrum of life. Zig used to say, we have five stages in life. We all start in "survival mode." Our parents take care of us because we can't yet take care of ourselves. Then we move from survival to "stability" as we learn to take care of ourselves. We might be in a new job or an apartment, just getting by. We move from stability to "success" as we learn our craft, get that promotion, and grow as a person. Up to this point in the process, we've been focused on making ourselves the best we can. But then, we go from success to "significance" by changing one key thing. It's a paradigm shift—when we move from helping ourselves, to helping other people climb to success. The last phase of life, he described as "Legacy." What will be your legacy? My story continues.

> We go from success to "significance" by changing one key thing. It's a paradigm shift—when we move from helping ourselves, to helping other people climb to success.

BE ALL THAT YOU CAN BE

I was able to get a bus ticket from San Louis Obispo to the downtown LA Greyhound station. From there, I walked a few blocks to get to the Los Angeles *Military Entrance Processing Station (MEPS)* where they processed me into the Army. That was an experience. They line you up with about 50 other guys and strip you down. They do a physical evaluation, and then you take an oath to serve. There is no turning back, you're in the Army now.

Part of the physical evaluation is a hearing test, and I was almost deaf in my right ear. I had infections growing up and eventually, as I said earlier, that led to surgery to remove my ear drum and corresponding bones. Dr. Guggenheim did the radical mastoidectomy procedure for me in Simi Valley when I was about nine-years old, and I had struggled with hearing loss ever since. Maybe this was one of the reasons I had such a hard time paying attention as a student. However, when I showed up at boot camp, that would not be a problem.

As I lined up and got off the bus at Ft. McClellan, Alabama, I was greeted by Drill Sergeant Murray. He was huge, intimidating, and very loud. "What the hell are you looking at, tick turd? Get your ugly ass into formation, GO, GO, GO!" he yelled as we exited the bus.

I was the smallest and the youngest guy in that formation. At 17, I was a whopping 5'5" and 125 pounds. A few days into the most brutal and painful experience of my life, Drill Sergeant Murray approached me and said, "Tick Turd, you need to be up there at 0800 a.m. to take the bus to the education center. I see here that you are one of the idiots I have that decided to drop out of high school. You will go and get your GED today; do you understand me, Private?"

"YES, DRILL SERGEANT!"

That was a long day. I was tested on a variety of subjects, and I don't ever remember a time when I was so nervous. That day, I passed the GED test and got my high school equivalent. I felt so proud of myself as only two of us passed the test. When I returned to my unit, Drill Sergeant Murray congratulated me and gave me the honor of wearing the Corporal stripes and put me in charge of my squad. An honor I soon found out was going to be more responsibility than I knew how to handle.

"First order of duty will be for your squad of maggots to clean the latrine, Dearing," Drill Sergeant Murray said. As I was in charge, I went to the guy I disliked the most and told him to clean toilets. He was a private like me, and he was in his late 20s. He was a bigger guy, over six feet tall, and had been picking on me in the previous days. He was now realizing I had pulled rank on him, and he wasn't about to let that happen. He said, "Hell no, I'm not doing that." So, I did what I thought was best, I reported him to the drill sergeant.

"He won't do what I told him to do drill sergeant," I said.

As the drill sergeant walked into the bathrooms with me, you could hear a pin drop. "Everyone understands that Dearing is in charge here, right?"

"Yes, drill sergeant!" all the men responded.

"Everyone drop and give me 20 pushups!" As we pushed, he said to the squad, "Anytime you knuckleheads don't listen, you'll push the ground until your arms fall off." Then he looked at me and said,

"You will do pushups every time anyone in your squad screws up. Do you understand me, Dearing?"

"Yes, drill sergeant!"

I didn't realize it at the time, but he was grooming me into a man because I did more pushups than anyone else in the platoon those two months. I grew five inches and gained thirty pounds in ten weeks.

I left Anniston, Alabama, for Fort Gordon, Georgia, that summer and learned how to climb telephone poles. It was the summer of '85 in Augusta, Georgia. The US Army had just opened the base to the Signal Corps, and I was one of the first to get on those telephone poles. We wore pole gaffs, huge spikes on our boots that allowed us to traverse to the top of the pole.

They had each of us put our paycheck up on the very top of the pole, then cover it with our hat. We would then have to climb down a few feet, reach left, reach right, and circle the pole before we could go back up to get the check. Motivation at its finest.

They taught us to push away so as not to get splintered on the way down. You also had to open your legs so you would not accidentally "gaff" yourself in the leg. One day I fell from the top of the pole. I hit the ground so hard on my rear end that I didn't think I was ever going to get back up that pole.

I had always been a crazy guy—no fear. I raced motorcycles and was an adrenaline junkie. But the Army put me in places that I feared, and I conquered those fears—one being a fear of heights. The team of soldiers who were in the same situation I was in made it possible for me to believe in myself. I left Fort Gordon in July of 1985 and flew to my next post in Frankfurt, Germany.

By the time I landed in Frankfurt, I was 18 years old and ready to explore what Europe was all about. I rode a train out to a small town called

Hoechst. I got off the train and rode my skateboard into McNair Kaserne and the 17th Signal Battalion. I was paired with a roommate named John from the Cincinnati area. He was a couple of years older than me, and almost as soon as we met, he became like a big brother to me.

"Hey Dude," I said.

"Dude?" he asked. "Where the hell are you from?"

"Los Angeles, California." I answered. "So how long you been here, John?"

"Long enough to know where to go to get drunk and to get laid," he told me.

I looked at him, smiled, and said, "I think we're going to get along, dude. Show me."

John and I tore up the town that first night. He said, "You know what *marks* are?"

"Marks? Yea," I said. "I have marks on my back from getting run over."

"No, *marks*. It's the money here, dumbass. Let's go get you some money."

He showed me the trains and how to get downtown. Then we went to an exchange so I could get some Deutsche Marks. The exchange rate in 1985 was 3 marks 50 pfennig to every dollar. This was huge for us soldiers because it meant our money was worth so much more, and it went a very long way.

As John and I navigated our way to the party spot in Frankfurt Sachsenhausen, we rolled into the Alabama Hard Rock bar. Apparently, John was already a legend there, because some GIs started yelling his name when we walked in.

As I sat down, I couldn't help but notice there were American men and German women everywhere. The old school jams at Alabama Hard Rock were hitting hard, I loved that place. John asked me if I'd ever had appflekorne. Of course I hadn't, so I asked him what the heck it was. He just told me that it's a drink that tastes like apple juice and ordered me one. Oh, it went down smooth and easy. I hadn't really been able to socialize or "party" at all during my training weeks, so I was ready for sure. I quickly became a fan of my first German brew. "This *apple corn* is killer, dude," I told John. About four hours later, we were in a cab on our way to Frankfurt Bier Haus.

What a place. There was a giant dance floor surrounded by tables. Upstairs, another circle of tables looked down on the dance floor. Every table had a phone and a giant number that you could light up or turn off.

"See those chicks over there?" John said, pointing to a table filled with young ladies. "Call their number and tell them to come over here." I did, and as they started to come our way, I couldn't help but notice the giant Adam's apple protruding from the neck of one of the girls. I quickly made sure she sat next to John. What a laugh we had that first night out on the town.

Bier Haus closed at 4 a.m., but the train didn't start running until 5 a.m., so John took me across the street to the "redlight" district. This area of town was seedy, dark, and a little sketchy to say the least, but then ahead of it was a well-lit, marble palace. It rose maybe 20 stories, and it was like a really high-end apartment building. This would be a night I would never forget. I had the gift of gab, and the German girls really liked me because my driver's license had my LA address on it. "Are you from Hollywood?" "Yes I am." I was learning new music, new fashion, and new dance moves every weekend.

I was having so much fun, I even picked up a side hustle working weekends as a disc jockey at the NCO club by my unit. It was an old-looking dive bar. Smokey rooms were filled with mauve-colored carpets that were covered with cigarette butt burns. The wood-paneled walls were lined with old slot machines. As bad as it looked, every Friday and Saturday night was a party. I was spinning rock on one side of the club and my boss, Mr. T, was spinning R&B on the other side.

It was pretty polarized racially back then. Most of the black soldiers would go to the R&B side and the people on the rock side were mainly white or Latino guys. Girls would go back and forth dancing and partying on one side then rocking out on my side. It was a recipe for old Stoner Joe to get back into some mischief. "Hey T, can you get me some blow and hashish?"

The drug of choice was LSD. They couldn't trace that in your system at the time, so didn't matter if you had to do a urine test or not. LSD was cheap and fun. I would trip all weekend and make money doing it. So many dumb things happened when I was with a group of buddies tripping. One night, Mike, Jerry, and I went out to Frankfurt on the train, tripping our minds out. Jerry was fascinated by the train as it was passing us in the station, so he said, "Hey guys, check it out." About that time, he fell into the side of the train and was thrown across the station, spinning like a top. I was like, "Holy shit!" and we just started laughing our asses off.

Jerry, however, was not laughing; his entire right side was a massive bruise. He could barely walk, but we got him back to the barracks. We laughed at him for months, but truth be told, someone was watching over us because he should have died in that train station, but instead, he walked away.

We were getting wasted almost every weekend unless we were in the field doing training exercises. I remember stealing a flashing road sign and taking it up to the barracks so I could trip and watch it blink all night. I then took it to the stairwell and left it on the first floor; I lived on the third floor. A little while later, I was in formation when I heard the Alpha company's first sergeant screaming at his men for putting a road light in the stairwell. They had to pull 24-hour stairwell guard duty for a month after. I never told a single person what I had done.

Another time, a group of us were tripping on LSD and went through a grave site. I got on my hands and knees and started digging up the ground on top of someone's grave. As I dug, I was howling and screaming like a ghost. Everyone took off running for their lives. It was a crazy time in my life, and I wasn't afraid of any possible consequences.

My preferred mode of transportation back then was my skateboard. I would ride out to the train station and catch the train or hang onto the back of a bus and ride behind it through town. Speaking of buses, I volunteered one day to go to bus driver training school. I was selected to be a bus driver for the summertime. I was to pick up children and take them to summer camp. I would literally sit there until they were ready to go to the public swimming pool. I was able to lounge freely, in uniform, of course, at the swimming pool every day.

The job was pretty cool, and I didn't have to show up for any formations that summer, so I was able to let my hair grow out quite a bit. I could stash it in my hat, and nobody could see that my hair was way out of regulation. I was able to crash at my friend Mike's house for the summer as well. He lived in an apartment in downtown Frankfurt only a couple of blocks away from the motor pool where my bus was located.

Living off campus in an apartment and growing my hair out made me fit in with the local scene much easier than the typical American GI. I was able to get into clubs that normally didn't allow American soldiers, and I was able to do things that most Americans couldn't do. I dated local German girls and wore clothes that made me fit in with the culture and the new wave scene that was popular there in the 80s. My time there was really fun, and then I did something foolish right before I left Germany.

With only two weeks left in the country, I drove the school bus and dropped off all my kids. Then I went to Mike's apartment to grab my skateboard. I stopped the bus, got out and ran up to get my board. I came back down and hopped back on the bus. As I was making my way out, I felt the right rear of the bus lift and thought to myself, *what was that?* I had run over the front of an Opal GT. I inspected the bus real fast and found that there wasn't a single scratch on it. I figured I would be gone in two weeks anyway, so I decided to take off. I got back to the motor pool and returned the bus in good condition. However, the guy with the crunched Opal GT saw the bus number and wrote it down.

I didn't know it, but in Germany, hit and run is a felony. When I returned to my barracks a few days later to out process, I was called into our commander's office. There stood three people who were all very disappointed: two German Polizei and my commanding officer. They began to tell me that I would not be leaving the country because of the hit and run incident unless I could pay for the damages right then and there. 1500 Marks, which at the time was around $500. I ran down the hall yelling out to everyone that I was selling my stereo system. I was able to conjure up the cash within a few minutes.

The good news was that got rid of the Polizei, the bad news: I was going to have to pull extra duty, working until midnight, every day that I remained in Germany. I also got what was called, "suspended bust." This meant when I showed up to my next assignment, I would have to continue pulling extra duty. The commander gave me an Article 15 (a quick way to punish soldiers who commit minor crimes) and demoted me from E4 back to E3. I left Germany as a Private First Class. Going backwards seemed to be my thing. I could always seem to find trouble wherever life took me. I had a month before I needed to show up for my next post, in Watertown, New York, so I took off for California.

When I got back to California, I purchased a VW bug for $50 and rebuilt it from the ground up. I remember standing on top of a mountain in Paso Robles at this body shop and smoking some cocaine out of a coke can. I never seemed to get out of my own way and the addictions that held me back from accomplishing great things. Even though I was in the Army, and even though I had the talent to build my own car, I was a mess and still an addict.

I left California and gave myself a week to drive that VW bug to New York. I stopped in Carthage, Missouri—which was about halfway— and visited my grandparents. My mom happened to be living there, so I was able to surprise her. I showed up at a local restaurant where she was a waitress and sat down in her section. As she approached the table, she just lit up with joy because she hadn't seen me in years. I was much taller, and she almost didn't recognize me at first. Our visit was brief; I departed for New York the next day.

As I was driving out of Carthage, I was fumbling around in my car looking for my lighter, and a large city truck stopped in front of me. I slammed into the back of it, and my head went into the windshield and shattered it. I got out and saw there wasn't a scratch on the truck, but the entire front end of my new VW bug was destroyed. I pulled the fenders out so I could turn the car, and I took off for New York. I could barely see out of the cracked windshield and only had one headlight, but I made it to my next assignment.

Watertown, New York. Home of Fort Drum and the 10th Mountain Division. This was the coldest place on the planet. When I showed up, I was already in hot water from the trouble that followed me from my last post, so I started with a negative balance for sure. One of the first things I was to do upon my arrival was to get a weapon. As I went to the arms room, a bus load of people was lined up to return their weapons. Lieutenant "Dooley" was the man in charge, and he was inspecting the weapons as the soldiers in my platoon cleaned them and turned them in.

I stood in line, and when I got up to the front, he asked where my weapon was. I told him I needed to get one assigned to me. He opened a crate and grabbed a brand new M16 out of the box. He said, "Clean this up and turn it in."

I looked it over and realized it was brand new and had never been fired. I wiped it off with some light oil and rammed a rod down the barrel to get any dust particles out. I stood in line again, and when it was my turn, Lt. Dooley looked at the weapon and said, "There is packing grease in the sights. Clean it up."

So, I cleaned it up and got back in line. Again, Lt. D looked at the weapon and said, "Did you even touch this thing? It's a mess! Clean it up!"

So I really took my time, I inspected every aspect of the weapon and determined the thing was spotless.

It was late Friday afternoon and already starting to get dark. I got the impression that the Lieutenant was not going to be able to get out of there until all the arms were locked up and secured, so I figured this time, he would definitely let me go. It was raining outside the large door, and there was a big mud puddle just outside. I was in the building but could see it was nasty and cold out there. I waited in line for the fourth time with my brand-new weapon and handed it to him. He looked at the butt of the weapon and told me it was dirty. At this point, I knew he had it in for me. It was probably because I was already in trouble before I even got there.

I said, "You are absolutely right, sir. This weapon is filthy." I then walked out into the rain and threw that brand new M16 into the mud puddle and sloshed it around. Lieutenant D completely blew a gasket. I don't believe I have ever seen anyone that pissed off in my life. I looked at him and said, "I guess I better clean this thing up, sir. You're right, it's a mess."

The lieutenant grabbed my arm and almost pulled it out of the socket. We went straight to my new commander's office. There was our Captain wondering what the hell was going on and who the hell was this new guy. Needless to say, I got another Article 15. I actually almost got kicked out of the Army that day.

I spent about two months on extra duty, and one day Lieutenant D showed up and said, "Congratulations Private, you are now going to be my personal driver. You will also be driving our platoon to the firing range since you have a bus driver's license. Oh, you're also going to be helping the firing squad whenever there is a funeral detail because they need a bus driver too."

Well, that didn't sound too bad. As part of my duties as his driver, I needed to have a top-secret security clearance so I could maintain the COMSEC. Communication security passcode and a decoding devise were around my neck at all times. I manned his personal radio, which was this giant, heavy thing that I had to take in and out of the Humvee and put into our tent.

I also had to put up his tent, cot, and heater. On top of that, I had to pull heater guard duty to ensure the tent didn't catch fire while he was asleep. Upstate New York is a miserably cold environment, especially when you're out in the field for 40 days during the winter. You can't get warm.

One day, I was driving him, and there were snow drifts on both sides of the road. He said, "Turn left."

I'm like, "Sir?"

He said, "Turn left."

"But sir," I replied, "There is no road."

He said, "Turn left now." So, I turned left into a snow drift and instantly buried the Humvee. He looked at me and said, "Grab your entrenching tool and dig us out."

The Army-issue entrenching tool was a shovel that folded up into the size of a sandwich, and it was something everyone had to carry. It would remove very little snow, so it literally took me over an hour to dig us out as he sat inside the warm vehicle. He hated me, and I hated him.

There was a field exercise, and we were to spend 40 days in the snow. It was brutal, we had to wash our underwear and dirty socks in our helmets. It was brutally cold in Watertown, New York. Late one evening, we were preparing to go to bed, and there were three or four feet of snow outside the tent. I went and got my section sergeant and asked him to pull fire guard so I could get some sleep. I'm not sure how much time passed, but I was asleep in my mummy bag (a sleeping bag used in extremely cold weather) and was awakened by something. As I looked out the little hole in my bag, I noticed the stars were bright. Then I remembered we were inside a tent, those weren't bright stars. My sergeant had fallen asleep, and the entire tent was on fire.

I woke up the sergeant and handed him a fire extinguisher. I grabbed the lieutenant's sleeping bag and pull it outside. He is like, "What the hell are you doing, Private?!" As he screamed at me, I was literally standing in three feet of snow—with only my underwear on.

I said, "The tent is on fire, sir! McDowell is putting it out." I ran back into the burning tent and got all the radio and COMSEC out of the tent. Then I fired up the Humvee.

When the Lieutenant figured out what was happening, he was like, "You saved my life! You saved all of the equipment." Meanwhile my sergeant said quietly, "You saved my ass." Needless to say, after that evening, the lieutenant and I were the best of friends, and I was promoted back to Specialist E4. The lieutenant also got me a letter of recognition from the brigade commander for saving him and all the equipment. I never told anyone that my sergeant was asleep, so he was also my new bestie. I never had to work much after that day.

When we returned from the field after surviving for 40 days and going through all of that with the fire, I was ready to cut loose. I got back, stripped off all my clothes leaving on only a pair of combat boots and tree gaff spikes. I walked through the snow outside my barracks and climbed up to the top of a telephone pole—completely naked. Everyone who was outside smoking started laughing at how crazy I was. It was a good time to remember, but it didn't last long.

About 6 months before I got out of the Army. I found out my mom needed a car, so I tried to fix up that old VW Bug for her. I got it running and went and purchased myself an '82 Camaro. My mom flew up to New York and drove that VW back down to Texas where she was living.

One night I packed my Camaro up with some friends, and we went into Watertown to grab some food and drinks. One of us had a bag of weed in the car, and we started into town. The passenger in the front seat saw a guy walking and said, "Hey, two points if you hit that guy." At that moment, he grabbed the steering wheel and pulled it towards the shoulder. He hit the pedestrian with the passenger side mirror and knocked him to the ground in the cold of the evening. Meanwhile, I oversteered back to the left, losing control of the car and ending up under an 18-wheeler that was parked on the side of the road. It all happened so fast. I looked at the guy in the shotgun seat and said, "What the hell did you do?"

I got out, grabbed a blanket out of the back of the car and ran to the poor guy lying in the road. I quickly went back to the car, found the weed, and hid it in the trailer of the 18-wheeler. The cops came and asked what happened, so I told them I had a flat and lost control. My car was totaled. I told the guy who had grabbed the wheel that he would be paying the deductible, but he never paid a dime. When I left New York, I still had a car payment on a $4,000 loan, but I had no car.

I was now out of the Army, broke, and had no car. I called my dad and said, "Hey man, can I come live with you in Cali for a few months?"

Thankfully, he said, "Nope," because I would have landed right back where I started.

I called my mom, and she said, "You can crash on my couch because that's all I've got." So, I moved back to Texas in April of 1989 and slept on my mom's couch for a few months. Turns out I didn't have to be in California to be Stoner Joe again. It wasn't long, and I was doing stupid things and getting in trouble again.

ADULTING

··

When I arrived in Texas, my mom said, "Well, I guess you can have your car back." I looked out into the parking lot and that old beat-up VW Bug was sitting there. She said, "It hasn't run in a couple months, I'm not sure why, but it won't start." I thought to myself *I guarantee it needs a set of points (an electronic part of the ignition system)*; I had it running that day. Of course, I still had to push-start the car to get it going, but it was better than walking.

I got into my mom's place and instantly found that the next-door neighbors were a couple of potheads who were my age. I went over there for a party one night and saw a young lady sitting on the couch. She was attractive, young, and looking at me, so I did what I always do—I sat right down and introduced myself. She was beautiful. I immediately asked her on a date. She had to be thinking I was a total loser when she saw I had to push-start my car. But within a few months, we were living together.

I had started a job working nights at Love Field Airport in Dallas. I got the job because I had top-secret security clearance in the Army. The job required high level security clearance because I was wiring avionics on multimillion dollar private business jets. The company I worked for was called KC Aviation, and I met some of the best people working there. One, a guy named Lance Heflin, I met on July 7, 1989. Today he is still one of my best friends. I loved the people but hated the job. It was relentless. I worked 18-hour days, 7 days a week. On the plus side, I got paid very well.

My girlfriend and I had been dating for only a few months when we decided to get married. We quickly went from renting to purchasing our first home in 1990. It was a small place in south Arlington, but it was ours, and I thought it was great because it had a pool and a garage so I could work on motorcycles. I soon started racing motocross out at Mosier Valley and Village Creek MX Park and was living life on the edge like I used to as a kid.

Motorcycles and getting dirty were part of my childhood and adolescence, and since I was making pretty good money, I felt like I should get back into that. It was my escape, my passion, and it was all I really wanted to do—go fast and jump far. Adrenalin rushed through my veins on Friday nights when I was out there racing. One night I felt like I could win this race, so I pinned it going off a jump and hit a kicker. As my rear tire went up my throttle got heavy, and I was in a panic revving that bike to try to bring it back down, but it was too far gone. I landed on my left shoulder, and my collar bone snapped. A short setback for me, but a few months after that my buddy Lance broke his collar bone on my dirt bike, so it was nice to already have the brace and the medication for him to use.

Meanwhile, my wife was working day shifts, and I worked nights, so we rarely saw each other the first year of our marriage. I remember going to a company picnic and seeing her socializing with one of the guys I worked with. I didn't really know the guy, but he made no secret about his desire to be around my wife. One night when I got off work at midnight, he asked if we would meet him at a bar to play some pool. I remember him coming around the backside of my wife and grabbing the pool stick while hugging her to show her how to hit the ball. It upset me because I didn't have the best self-esteem. Anyway, I wrote it off to jealousy and tried not to hang out with him much. We hadn't even been married a year yet, so I wasn't thinking she wasn't doing anything inappropriate with the guy. She eventually told me that she was "in love" with him, but that "nothing" ever happened. I was glad when he moved away, but I always suspected something was going on.

She worked for a guy who was a doctor in the family medicine business. She was an insurance billing clerk. The doctor was young and handsome and was very wealthy. He owned a very large house and a Porsche. One day at a Christmas party for her work, he pulled me aside and asked, "Can you score me some cocaine?"

I said, "Yeah, how much do you want?"

He said, "I need an ounce per week." That is a lot of coke, but I quickly found the supply chain and went to work because I figured this dude would pay whatever I would charge him. At the time, in 1991, an ounce of cocaine cost me $800, so I would charge him $1600 an ounce, and I would buy two ounces. I quickly became very successful selling my other ounce for almost twice as much, selling it in smaller quantities. Every week I was either making $800 cash or buying myself an ounce of cocaine to sell for even more than that.

I was running a risk but had it down to a weekly routine, and I was making some serious cash. One day I asked the doctor what type of services he farmed out to a third party, and he told me about vascular ultrasound. I asked if I could sit in on a procedure to see what it was that they did in his office. A guy showed up with a machine, checked for a pulse with this doppler device and took some blood pressure readings with the cuffs. Then he had a radiologist read the reports that were produced. The doctor would bill the insurance, and I would charge the doctor for leasing the equipment and my time. I thought to myself, I can do this.

I worked nights at the airport, and then would get up early and study vascular ultrasound. I took a two-week vacation to go to a training seminar nearby in Las Colinas that taught the principles of vascular ultrasound. I was certified to do vascular in a couple of weeks. It really wasn't much different than the hydraulics in an automobile; I had it figured out quickly. I had been saving all that cash, so I purchased an ultrasound machine, and just like that, Mobile Medical Services (MMS)—my mobile ultrasound company—was born.

Mobile Medical Services was launched during the day, and I worked my job at the airport every night. I also kept selling cocaine. I was cashing in, and one day I decided to quit the night job. That was a bad move for a few reasons, not least of which was because that was who I had insurance through. By this time, my wife was pregnant, so I opted to pay the $800 per month Cobra plan for insurance in case something happened during her pregnancy. Also, I had only a few doctors lined up doing ultrasound with my company, and my wife's boss was one of them. I started to fall short on the bills and really needed to do something that was a sure paycheck.

I searched around for other mobile imaging companies and found a company called MASI. A man named Bruce Hammond was there, and he was from California, so we immediately clicked. He was a very smart and successful Christian man. He said, "I tell you what, you can sell me your machine and your few doctors' accounts, and I will bring you on as my vascular tech. But I don't have a ton of vascular work here, so you will also need to do other things to help the operation."

I did everything for this guy, he was awesome. I answered phones, scheduled exams, got up at 4 a.m. to deliver radioactive isotopes to different hospitals, and yes, I even did vascular ultrasound every now and then. Bruce's company was a big provider of mobile nuclear medicine in most of Texas at the time. One day, I went to Comanche, Texas, to do an ultrasound on a 96-year-old lady who had gangrene on both legs all the way up to her knees. As she laid curled up, she moaned in pain, and she smelled like death. It was the smell of rotting flesh.

The doctor on duty there handed me a Sharpie pen and said, "Listen to the doppler and make an X on both legs where the blood flow stops."

I did as I was told and marked two big x's on each of the woman's legs just above the knees. I said, "Hey doc, what's up with the x's?"

He said, "That's where we will be cutting off both of her legs."

I went to work the next day and told Bruce that I didn't want to do vascular ultrasound anymore, so he said, "Ok, you are now my new sales rep. Go sell something." This was the beginning of my turn around. I was a natural sales guy because I was able to make friends with people pretty quickly. But this Cali boy found that trying to sell in rural Texas was a little challenging.

"Hey Bruce, who is the kid with the plastic hair and the ponytail who's coming out here trying to sell me something?"

"That's California Joe," he would tell them.

My wife was very pregnant with our first son, and she was about to give birth any day. She was scheduled to be induced on June 8, and it was around May 15 when I called in on a local radio station contest and won eight tickets to a rock festival over the Memorial Day weekend—which happened to fall on my birthday that year. Man, I was excited! I invited all my best buds to go with me. Lance and my brother-in-law and a few others were there to party. I showed up with a case of Foster's lager in the trunk, a bunch of cocaine, and my brother-in-law had some weed. We tailgated in the parking lot and started to catch a buzz for the concert.

Not sure where everyone went, but at some point, I was playing hacky sack with a group of guys when I decided to do this big jump spin move to kick the hacky sack. I landed wrong on my left foot and snapped my tibia and fibula. I sat down and started to vomit. My buddies came and got me and were like "now what?" I said, "Let's party dudes." We stayed all day and all night at the concert and then went to a party after the show. I was totally hammered the entire time because I was in so much pain.

The next day I realized, "Damn, my ankle is swollen and black and blue!" My nine-months-pregnant wife was wondering what the hell happened. I went and got an x-ray and found that both bones were broken. I decided I'd wait until the baby came and then have my surgery done. June 8, we went to the hospital so she could give birth. They worked for hours trying to get him out. My wife was in massive pain as she struggled with him.

When he came out, he was purple. "Oh, that's normal," the nurse said. But he was still purple after a few minutes, so they checked his o2 level and realized he had no oxygen. They put him in an incubator and flew him to Children's Hospital in Dallas. The helicopter took him away right after he was born. He was diagnosed with transposition of the great vessels. His aorta and pulmonary arteries were transposed so oxygenated blood was going back to his lungs and deoxygenated blood was circulating through his body. They had to do something, and they had to do it fast.

Meanwhile, I was still sitting in Grand Prairie with a broken leg, and my wife was covered in blood. I told her, I guess I will see you after my surgery. On June 9, all three of us were in different hospitals at the same time. My son was at Children's, I was in south Dallas, and my wife was in Grand Prairie. What a day to remember. I got out of bed and noticed some hemovac thing coming out from a cast on my leg. I pulled it out, then put my street clothes on, and walked out of the hospital with some nurse yelling at me to come back.

I got a ride to Children's in Dallas and found my son. By this time, they had stabilized him with drugs to keep his vessels open and a hormone to make his body think he was still in the womb, which kept another blood vessel open for him. They pumped vaso dilators and oxygen into him for three days. By the time my wife and I were both able to get to Children's, medical personnel were hauling him off to do open heart surgery. It was a very tough time for our young family for sure.

Our son came out of surgery bloated up like a cabbage patch doll. He was full of fluid and swelling. He had tubes in his arms, legs, and chest cavity. It was sad to watch, but every day he looked better and better. After a few weeks, we were able to take him home, but he did not know how to suckle or eat on his own, so I had to put a naso-gastric tube in his nose to feed him for those first couple of weeks. I was very thankful for that Cobra insurance policy I had been paying $800 a month for. It picked up the entire tab for my wife's delivery, my son's open-heart surgery, and my broken leg. Just want to say that my firstborn son turned 30 this year, and the people who saved his life are amazing. Thank you, Dr. Leonard for saving my son's life.

It's like July, and I told my boss I was coming back to work. I had been off for almost a month. But Bruce said, "No, you need to be with your family. But don't worry, I will continue to pay you." He paid me for two months. Bruce had a heart of gold, and he was a real father figure to me. He was praying for us every day, and I had no idea who this God was that he was praying to. I never really believed in God; I had been to church a few times in my life but not really because I wanted to go.

When you are a drug addict, and life throws you the kind of stress I had experienced, you usually go back to doing more drugs. That is exactly what I did. I went back to the doctor I had sold coke to and asked him if he needed more. He said he sure did, so I provided it—only this time, it was different. This time, my wife who had never done drugs in her life, decided it would help her to lose weight, and she started doing cocaine with me and her doctor boss. One thing led to another, and we both started partying with the doctor at his house.

We had a baby, but we didn't let that stop us from doing a bunch of coke. One day, I came home early from a sales trip and could not find my wife. I stopped at her work, but they said she had left. I went home, but she wasn't there. I decided to see if she was at the doctor's house, and there was her car right in the driveway. I called the doctor from the big bag phone that I had in my work car. He answered the phone and told me he hadn't seen her all day. As I was down the road from his house, looking at my wife's car, I thought to myself, "Just ram this car right into his house."

I went home and got drunk. When my wife showed up at about 10 p.m., she said, "Oh you're home early!"

I'm like, "Yeah, where you been?"

"Oh, I had to work late."

I told her I knew all about her and the doctor, but she said nothing happened between them. But, as far as I was concerned, our marriage was over. I walked out and got my own place and started seeing other women.

I really started racing a lot during that time. I even moved up to north Arlington close to Mosier Valley where I loved to race. I lived recklessly—seeing women and racing dirt bikes. Eventually, I moved back home because my wife couldn't afford to live there on her salary and had moved into an apartment.

I did what I had to do at work, but I was really getting skinny from all the drugs and constant partying. One day, Bruce pulled me aside and said, "We need to talk." In a stern voice he said, "You've got so much potential, but you're wasting it. I know what you're doing, you're not fooling anyone," he said. "It's time for a come-to-Jesus meeting."

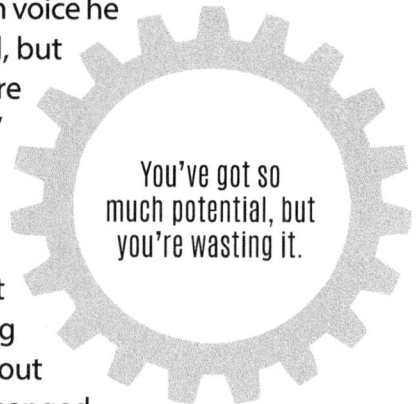

> You've got so much potential, but you're wasting it.

I was scared because I didn't want to lose my job on top of everything else. He sat with me and told me about Jesus Christ and how the Lord had changed his life. We talked about my marital issues and drug usage. He then offered me an ultimatum: clean up my act or find another place to work. He then told me he loved me and that's why he wouldn't watch me destroy myself anymore. It was a real "come-to-Jesus" meeting alright. He stepped up and shared something with me that day that would change my life.

I left that meeting with Bruce and went home. I was depressed and felt like I had lost it all, so I grabbed my gun and put it to my head. I was crying and telling myself to do it, just end it. Then I fell to my knees and started bawling my eyes out. I spoke to God and said, "If you are real, could you help me out?" I felt a tingling sensation fill my body. I felt a peace come over me, and I put the gun down. I wiped the tears away and said, "Ok, I'm going to quit doing drugs right now." I took what I had and flushed them down the toilet, and for three days I fought with myself in that house. I broke things, put holes in the walls, and on the third day, I went to church by myself. It was like God was speaking directly to me that day. I asked Jesus to be my lord and savior that day.

Literally the same day, the guy who I had been buying my drugs from came to my house. He walked in and threw a bag of cocaine on my coffee table and said, "Dude, where you been hiding?"

I said, "I've been here, and I want you to know that Jesus loves you, and he can change your life." I never saw that guy again. He left that day and never came back.

I went to my wife's apartment and sat at her doorstep until she came home, and I asked her if she would move back into the house. My son was probably six months old at the time, and my wife really needed help. I told her I had cleaned up my act and started going to church. She decided to do the same, and we started over. We were very active in the church. I met some very nice people and even picked up a new mentor—the man who was leading our Sunday school class.

One day, I shared my story with him, and he asked if I would share my testimony with the congregation. This church was massive. Fielder Road Baptist Church in Arlington, Texas, was huge. There were three services back-to-back, and I shared my story in all three. Countless young people came to the front to accept Christ into their lives, and for the first time in my life, I actually felt significant. It was like I was here and went through all that for a reason. The reason was to help other people.

My entire life was changing. Bruce sold the business to a much larger, publicly held company, and I went to work for a guy named Mark Foley. Mark was the senior vice president of sales for the new company, DHS. He was a killer sales guy. He began to influence my sales career and provided me resources from people like Zig Ziglar to help me with my sales technique. I was listening to tapes in the car, reading books, and doing everything I could to be the best sales guy I could be.

To give you an idea, I made around $30,000 working for MASI, and I started making over $100,000 working for DHS. My career was taking off, and I was being blessed beyond measure in many different areas in life. My wife and I had another son in 1997. I must say, I was a little worried, but this time was different. My second son came into the world without any health issues. Not only that, but now, my wife could stay home to raise the kids because I was making good money.

One day in 1999, Mark Foley said, "Hey, DHS is going to be delisted from NASDAQ because they have been doing some bad accounting practices. My friends Michael Norton, Frank Singer, and I want you to come with us and do something called SalesRepsOnline. It's a website that caters to salespeople." I was all for it.

TWO DUDES RACING

It was the dotcom boom, and everything was going to an internet platform, including salesforce automation. At the time, most CRM solutions were thick client software applications that had to be downloaded on your PC. To avoid the hardware and software obsolescence factor SalesRepsOnline partnered with a brand-new company, Salesforce.com.

We offered the Salesforce automation tools, but we had additional content on our site that catered specifically to helping salespeople generate and close more business. We partnered with big names like Zig Ziglar, Tom Hopkins, Denis Waitley, and Miller Heiman, to name a few. We had hours of their content on how to overcome objections and how to close a deal right there in the same space as the pipeline forecasting and other sales support, like booking travel.

Our timing was perfect, but before we really were able to get going, a software giant named Tom Seibel purchased the company. Seibel was known for having the most expensive and robust CRM software solutions available. Tom Seibel had worked for Larry Ellison at Oracle but broke away because he really believed the CRM customer relationship management platform that he developed would change the world. He purchased SalesRepsOnline and turned it into Sales.com.

I became a passionate student of the sales process and tried to leverage that into some big accounts for our team. I remember flying out to Rochester, New York, to do a huge presentation for the company Paychex. Up until now, I had been selling to only small, rural hospitals and doctors' offices, and I was really growing my sales game. My sales quota was enormous, and I was trying my hardest to make everything work. I traveled a lot. I was almost never home, but my wife was home with the kids, so I knew I could just focus on selling and trying to provide for them.

In 2000, I sold our little house that we had lived in for 10 years and purchased a big house out on Lake Arlington. It was a very nice place, and since we were on the lake, we bought a boat. I also purchased a new Ford Explorer to pull the boat and my motorcycle trailer. Life was going really good until I got a call from Michael Norton telling me I had been laid off. In fact, we had all been laid off.

Michael told me that the Sales.com product was cannibalizing the Seibel mid-market software product, so they cancelled us. Looking back on it, it's probably the worst decision Seibel ever made because Salesforce.com ran them over and took the entire market. Meanwhile, the country was going through a recession, and I was having trouble finding another job. I had been racing dirt bikes every weekend with my sons and working on other kids' bikes, so I decided to start my own motorcycle shop , and *Two Dudes Racing* was born.

Two Dudes was the coolest little shop for kids who wanted to race dirt bikes. I sold Cobra and Polini Motorcycles, Redline BMX bicycles, I had GoPed scooters, and Carter Go-carts. I also had a full-blown skateboard shop. It was a legendary kids' paradise.

We purchased a 38-foot trailer to do trackside support. We did performance modifications to make the fastest little bikes in town, and my two boys were fast. We spent every weekend racing somewhere. We did all the Nationals including Ponca City and Loretta Lynn's. We cleaned up at all the local races, and we also had our own race team. We were spending more money than we could make, but we were having the time of our lives. I used racing to teach my kids how to be competitive, prepared, and on their game.

If you ever want to make a small fortune in the motorcycle business, you'll need to start with a *large* fortune. I spent two years trying to grow *Two Dudes* into a profitable business, but we were burning through our saving at a fast rate. I had asked my wife to find work to help us make ends meet since both of our children were in school at this point. She refused to do anything to add to our income other than sitting up at the shop all day. The problem with that is she didn't know how to sell a motorcycle or fix one, so the shop was doomed and so were we, as she just didn't do anything to help make us money.

After burning through our savings, the bank foreclosed on my new lake house. It was auctioned off, and I lost every penny of equity I had put into it. Then they repossessed my new truck, so I purchased an old beater truck, and we rented an old house behind the shop. I did everything I could to stay in business, but even after all that, my wife would not go find any work. I reached out to my old friend Michael Norton who was working at a new start up—MD Data Corp.

Funny story, Michael had set up an interview for me at the DFW airport. I lived about 30 minutes south of the airport in Mansfield, so I figured no worries I can meet them during their layover and do the interview. I woke up and there was ice hanging from my house. My diesel truck did not want to start because it needed glow plugs and it had a dead battery. I decided to ride a motorcycle to the airport. I put on a nice suit and tie, fired up one of the street bikes I had for sale and began my journey to DFW airport in the freezing cold weather. I got to the airport and the guys could not believe that I went through all that just to meet with them. I showed up with icicles coming out of my nose like the guys on dumb and dumber. Needless to say, I got the job and went to work for them, but it was short lived. I ended up moving the shop to a cheaper space and kept trying to fix bikes on weekends and after my work hours, but it was doomed. I literally had nothing left.

I called my old friend Bruce Hammond in 2002, and he offered me another shot at DHS as the North Texas sales rep. I took it. I was able to get something going, but not before I had to file bankruptcy and close the doors at *Two Dudes*. I just couldn't do both jobs at the same time. It was a lost cause. My dream of having my own business was crushed, and I blamed it on my wife for not getting a job. I had some serious resentment going on. In fact, I would say that I literally hated her at the time because she just sat there and watched everything get taken away and did nothing.

During those last couple of years during the *Two Dudes Racing* years, I started to get the wondering eye. I had been wanting to explore new relationships with different women. I was looking for trouble, and it found me. I was losing interest in my wife and really was not in love anymore. I would try to find a hook up here and there as I traveled. I wasn't faithful to her those last couple of years, but I always tried to rationalize my behavior, saying I was doing it because of the things she had done in the past. Our marriage was pretty much done when I filed for bankruptcy. I was only there for my kids at that point.

One day Bruce said, "Hey, I need you to go to Oklahoma. We are closing an office up there, and we fired the division manager. I need you in Tulsa to get a sales plan for that area. We need more nuclear medicine sales up there, and you need to build it."

So, I went to Tulsa, Oklahoma, on September 9, 2002, for a staff meeting. I didn't know anyone in the Oklahoma division very well.

When I got there it was already a full room. Our DM from Texas— Barbara—was there, and one of the first people I met that night was a beautiful woman named Tammie Hodgson. She was 27, had a big smile, and she was beautiful. She was welcoming people as they came in the door. When it was my turn, I gave her a big hug and introduced myself. Someone noticed that we didn't have refreshments, so I offered to go pick some things up, and Tammie went with me.

I got to know Tammie on a very personal basis as we often traveled together for medical staff meetings. I guess both of us were in the same boat at the time and had a listening ear. She had recently had to file for bankruptcy too, so I guess misery loves company. A few months after Tammie and I became intimate with each other, she decided she ought to quit the job and focus on trying to fix her marriage up in Oklahoma.

I ended up selling the inventory at the shop for pennies on the dollar and walked away from *Two Dudes Racing*. I moved to central Texas for a change and to try to keep my family together, but it wasn't long after that my wife and I divorced. She moved farther south to the San Antonio area, so I found a house near her so I could help raise our boys. She was a very kind and good woman. She did not deserve to be treated the way I treated her. It just didn't work out.

I was still working for Bruce at DHS, but around mid 2005, my entire life changed. This is another step in my turning point. I was broke, divorced, had no credit, no money, and I had lost my family. I was officially a complete disaster. I had lost everything. And then, I got a call from my old friend and mentor Michael Norton. He was working at the Zig Ziglar Corporation and asked me if I would join him there as a sales guy.

When I got there, I met Zig and his son Tom. The Ziglar people were an amazing group of hard-working professionals. We started the week off every Monday morning with a devotional. Every now and then, Zig would lead, it but if not, there were always some very smart and successful people there to do it. I learned how to teach all of our classes. I got certified on "Strategies for Success," "The Selling Difference," "Presentation Skills," "Goal Setting and Achieving." Every single course Zig Ziglar had written, every book, tape and CD was going into my head. "You are what you are and who you are by what goes into your mind." –Zig Ziglar

You are what you are and who you are by what goes into your mind. -Zig Ziglar

One day, I was walking down the hall at our Dallas office, and as I was passing Zig, he stopped me and asked a unique question, "Are you a wondering generality or a meaningful specific?" What he was asking was, did I have a plan or was I just kind of flying by the seat of my pants. He was onto me, so I got a plan and decided to work my life according to the plan.

I really started to internalize the information I had been given over the months I had been working there. He had a philosophy that changed my life in every area, and I'm going to spend the next several chapters explaining this philosophy so it can change yours too. It starts with your "Wheel of Life."

Are you a wondering generality or a meaningful specific?

WHEEL OF LIFE

In 1920, Stanford University embarked on a study of 1440 genius-level youngsters. The researchers followed these individuals for their life. When the man who initiated the research retired, the study was continued by his department. Here is what they found: most of the subjects became outstanding successes not because of their genius, but rather, because of their ability to focus on what was important and then persist until they reached their goal. This means that setting goals is essential to success. Having a roadmap to follow will help you get where you want to go. So how do we start to plan our life's ambitions and desires?

When Zig asked me the question "Are you a wondering generality or a meaningful specific," I know he was really asking, *Do you have a roadmap to success? Do you have a plan? Do you set goals?*

Do you have a roadmap to success? Do you have a plan? Do you set goals?

Everyone wants to be happy, healthy, prosperous, secure, and have healthy relationships, peace of mind, and hope for the future. The question is this, if you want these things, have you identified them as goals and written them down? If not, how do you expect to get what you want in life?

Have you developed a plan of action and set a completion date to achieve that plan? Happiness, like money, is the result of what you do. If you know that you are using the ability that you have, then your chances of being happy are dramatically improved. Everything you have is a direct result of who you are and what you do, and everything you want is outside of your comfort zone.

There are four reasons that people do not have or use a goals' program.

> Everything you want is outside of your comfort zone.

- The first reason is FEAR. False Evidence Appearing Real.

A lot of times we believe we *can't* do something or we're afraid of failing. Zig always said, "Failure is an *event*, not a *person*." Don't be afraid to fail. Your "failure to launch" is all in your head, so lose the limited image you have of yourself and try to do something new. It is dangerous for a ship to leave the harbor, but it is more dangerous for the ship not to move and, instead, rust out. We need to fuel our confidence with a belief in ourselves that allows us to leave the harbor rather than sit and get rusty. Here is a fact: you will miss every shot that you don't take.

> Failure is an event, not a person.

How do you see yourself? Dr. Joyce Brothers said, "You cannot consistently perform in a manner that is inconsistent with the way you see yourself." Change the picture you have of yourself, and you can change your performance.

- The second reason for not having goals is a poor self-image.

What do you think of you? If you think you can or if you think you can't—you're right. Do you see yourself as valuable and important, or do you see yourself as a failure? Self-image is a big thing that has so much bearing on whether or not you are going to achieve success in any area of your life. You were designed for accomplishment, engineered for success, and endowed with the seeds of greatness.

The truth is this, people who take immediate action when they first hear the concept of a goals' program are ten times more likely to do something about it. When directions are set and commitments are made, almost immediately, help will come to your aid to assist you in accomplishing those goals. The people around you want to see you accomplish great things, and as soon as you get going, they will want to go with you.

- The third reason that people don't set goals is because they have never been sold on the concept.

The thing here is that taking the time to plan your life and take deliberate action to improve in all areas is really as simple as figuring out what you want to *Be, Do,* or *Have* and then writing down your action plan to improve in all those areas. If you don't believe that having a plan for your life will help you get there, then you haven't been sold on the concept.

Many people have goals but are not sure how to set them properly.

- The fourth reason people don't write down their goals is because they just don't know how to start using a goals' program. That, my friends, is why I wrote this book.

Let's look at Zig Ziglar's *Wheel of Life*. This is a simple process which identifies the key areas in your life that need the most work. You will see that each "Spoke" on the wheel is an area that you want to improve on. I have taken this concept and put it to work to influence and grow in all areas of my life. This is the key to identifying your strengths and weaknesses. Look at the wheel closely and you will see each Spoke is numbered from one to ten. Go ahead and grade yourself in each area on the wheel. You might have some categories that need more work than others, so you might be a three right now.

But in other areas, you might be stronger—like an eight. Go ahead and grade yourself in each area, then connect the dots.

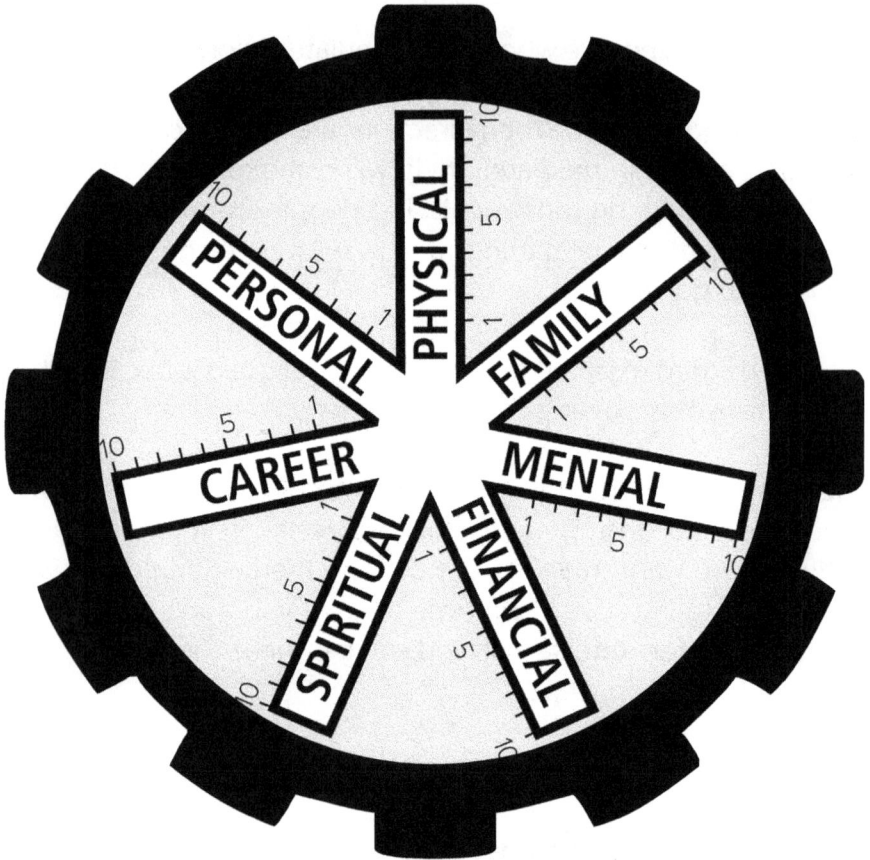

Your wheel might look like a bumpy ride but that shows where you should focus your energies first. The idea is to have balance in your life as well as growing your wheel. Right now, your wheel might be small, but take the time to fill it out to determine where you are currently in each Spoke.

I will go through each Spoke later in the book and share what I did to achieve great success in every Spoke. Take the time to write down everything you want to *Be, Do,* or *Have* in the space below.

BE	DO	HAVE

Notes:

....

....

....

....

....

....

....

....

....

....

....

....

....

....

....

....

....

....

....

....

....

....

....

Doing both exercises should produce a few goals that you can start with. Once you get the system working for you, you can take the same approach with every goal, in every Spoke. You are going to be unstoppable as you begin to see the results from having a well-balanced plan in place that works. Before we set goals, we need to ask ourselves a few qualifying questions.

1. Is this really my goal?
2. Is my goal morally right and fair to everyone concerned?
3. Is this consistent with my other goals?
4. Can I emotionally commit myself to finishing the goal?
5. Can I see myself reaching the goal?
6. Does it meet the requirements of the basic eight?

Using this as your guide, you can be assured that the goal you are setting is going to be beneficial to you and others. Now you may be asking, what is the *basic eight*? The basic eight is the following eight questions. If you can answer *yes* to any of them, then you have a realistic goal, and you are ready to put it on paper and develop the action plan to accomplish it.

- Will it make me happier?
- Will it make me healthier?
- Will it make me prosperous?
- Will it make me more secure?
- Will it help me make more friends?
- Will it give me better family relationships?
- Will it give me more peace of mind?
- Will it increase my hope for the future?

There are characteristics of goals. Some goals are big—seem out of reach, but not out of your sight—to make you stretch and grow to your maximum potential. Other goals are long range. Some goals will need to be broken down and analyzed to determine where you are and what steps need to be taken. You should also have daily goals to keep your discipline and stay focused on the details of your daily life. Your goals need to be specific so you can envision them more easily. Some goals are ongoing because they are part of a process (i.e., losing weight etc.). I will highlight my experience with implementing this philosophy in the coming chapters.

The first time I did my *Wheel of Life* was in 2005 while I was working at the Ziglar offices in Dallas. Here were my results the first time I graded myself (remember, I was a mess and had pretty much lost everything when I was introduced to this concept).

Spiritual Spoke: 1 – I was living in sin, not going to church, or reading my Bible at all. But hey, at least I was a Christian, so I gave myself a 1.

Family Spoke: 2 – I lost my wife to divorce, and my kids were now living with her.

Mental Spoke: 2 – I was always learning new things, but the fact was, I was a high school dropout with no real formal education.

Career Spoke: 5 – I was working for Zig Ziglar, so my career wasn't so bad, but I had just closed my shop and lost everything in the process.

Financial Spoke: 1 – I had just filed for bankruptcy.

Physical Spoke: 3 – I was about 50 pounds overweight.

Personal Spoke: 4 – Not sure why I gave myself a 4 on this, but I guess I figured I had a few areas in my life that weren't that bad.

Not only did I have a very small "wheel," but it was way out of balance, and my life was a bumpy road—as my wheel indicated. (Spoiler alert, I made massive improvements in every Spoke and have had tremendous success as a result of developing a plan for my life and executing the plan.)

I started my journey with the *Family Spoke*. Now, you can prioritize your wheel however you see fit, and you can work on more than one Spoke at a time if you want, but I decided to take each Spoke in order of my priorities, and I did one thing at a time.

It has been said "If you are chasing two rabbits, you will not catch either one," so I got very specific in each Spoke and spent a year developing that area. The next year, I would pick a different *spoke* on my *Wheel of Life*. The chapters in this book are laid out in the order that I set and accomplished my goals, but you can tailor the order to fit your program.

FAMILY SPOKE

Y ou have already read about my childhood and all the crazy things I did to annoy my parents along the way. You also know that I got married, had two boys, and was not the best husband to my first wife. I cheated on her, I was a drug-addicted fool, and I put her through a lot. We ended up divorced, and my family was left broken, so I want to start the lesson with the *Family Spoke*.

Being divorced, I only saw my kids half the time—they were with their mother for a week, then I had them for a week—so, I had some work to do on my Family Spoke. I was very engaged in my children's development and extracurricular activities; I supported their desire to take drum lessons and join the middle school band. (Both of my boys are amazing drummers now.) I had always been a great dad. We did motorcycle racing, t-ball, coach-pitch baseball, drums, you name it, I was all in it with them, and I didn't want that to stop because of a divorce. I was making the best of it, but then something happened that would change my family life for the better.

I had been alone for a while, so I called my friend Tammie. A mutual friend had told me that she had ended up divorced as well. I wanted to see what, if any, interest was there because the two of us had become very close, and I missed her. We reconnected right away. The big problem was I was living in New Braunfels, Texas, and she lived in Moore, Oklahoma, about seven hours away, with her five-year-old daughter.

Tammie and her daughter came down to New Braunfels for a visit, and it went very well. A few months later, they moved to Texas to start a life with me and the boys. Tammie got an apartment about a mile away from my home, and we began to date like normal folks. After about six months, Tammie and her daughter moved in with us, and we got married in 2006. I was trying to build my family unit back to a place that resembled something normal for our children.

As I developed my Family Spoke, I felt like the relationship between my kids and me was better—until they became teenagers—and I stayed plugged in to their activities so they would know that I would always be there for them. I never missed a performance or a game during their combined eight years of high school band. And even though I couldn't stand the smell, I helped my little girl raise ten pigs during her four years in the Future Farmers of America (FFA) program at her school.

I was also able to be there when they came home from school to help with homework or with any challenging situations they might have been dealing with that day. My daughter would come home upset from time to time, and I would always take her for ice cream so we could talk about it. After a while, she caught onto me, and she came home "upset" three times a week. The guy at the Baskin-Robbins ice cream joint knew us both by name because we were there so much.

While I was at it, I also took the time to try to make a better connection with my dad. I needed to forgive him for some things. I doubt that I would have gone there had it not been for the spiritual side reminding me that *I* was forgiven so I should also be forgiving to *others*. Besides that, you can't carry a grudge against someone knowing he was just a young man with an addiction problem decades ago. Let it go, man. I rode my Harley from San Antonio to his home in Ruidoso, New Mexico, a distance of 635 miles. He and I rode together to Colorado, back down through the Great Divide, into Taos, and then back to his place. That was over 600 miles per day for two more days, then I dropped him off and rode home. Four days of riding over 2500 miles. It was great.

My dad recently left my house following a short visit, and it was clear he couldn't be prouder of me. I was able to take my Family Spoke from a *one* to an *eight*. I still have one family relationship to work on and that is with my sister. My sister and I have been through a lot over the years. We both have trauma in our lives that we've had to try to deal with, and we both went to drugs for relief. In time, my plan is to have a happy family that knows I'm always there for them.

Working on family, marriage, and kids, all of these are great areas in which to set some goals if you feel like you've been absent or did something that really had a negative impact on their lives. Reconnect—make it a priority, and you will see results. Your family will thank you for it down the road as my children did.

> Reconnect—make it a priority, and you will see results. Your family will thank you for it down the road as my children did.

My boys think I'm the best dad even though I made mistakes in my first marriage. My wife Tammie loves me dearly even though I'm not always the most lovable person. In fact, it is her support and willingness to help me that got me through the rest of these Spokes, and I have to tell you, I was able to get a lot done having her as my partner, friend, and mentor. We have built a wonderful life together and have been happily married for over 16 years now. All the kids are grown and have moved out. I just hope they set goals for their families, so they don't end up in a failed marriage like I did.

What about you and your family? Wouldn't you like to have close relationships with them? Would you like to restore relationships that might have been damaged because of something that happened in your past? What kind of baggage are you lugging around in resentment and unforgiveness towards someone in your family? Maybe it's time to get rid of the things that are keeping you from having wonderful relationships with your family members.

Improving family relationships requires effort, communication, and understanding from all members involved. Here are some steps you can take to foster better family relationships:

1. **Open and Honest Communication**: Encourage open communication among family members. Create a safe space where everyone feels comfortable expressing their thoughts, feelings, and concerns.
2. **Active Listening**: Practice active listening when others are speaking. Give your full attention, refrain from interrupting, and try to understand their perspective without judgment.
3. **Empathy and Understanding**: Show empathy and understanding towards each other's experiences and emotions. Put yourself in their shoes to better comprehend their feelings.
4. **Resolve Conflicts Respectfully**: Conflicts are normal in any family, but how they are handled can make a significant difference. Resolve conflicts calmly and respectfully, avoiding blame and criticism.
5. **Quality Time Together**: Make an effort to spend quality time as a family. Participate in activities that everyone enjoys and create positive memories together.
6. **Set Boundaries and Respect Privacy**: Respect each other's boundaries and privacy. Understand that individuals need space and time to themselves.
7. **Share Responsibilities**: Distribute household and family responsibilities fairly among family members. Encouraging everyone to contribute fosters a sense of teamwork and mutual support.

8. **Celebrate Each Other's Successes**: Celebrate each other's achievements and milestones. Be supportive and encouraging of individual growth and accomplishments.

9. **Forgiveness and Letting Go**: Practice forgiveness when family members make mistakes. Holding onto grudges can damage relationships, so let go of past conflicts and move forward.

10. **Avoid Comparison**: Refrain from comparing family members to each other. Each person is unique, with their strengths and weaknesses, and should be appreciated for who they are.

11. **Respect Differences**: Embrace and respect each other's differences, including differing opinions, beliefs, and personalities.

12. **Family Meetings**: Hold regular family meetings to discuss important topics, make decisions together, and address any concerns.

13. **Support During Tough Times**: Offer support and be there for each other during challenging times. Show compassion and kindness when family members are going through difficulties.

14. **Express Love and Affection**: Don't hesitate to express love and affection to your family members regularly. Verbalize your feelings and demonstrate care through actions.

15. **Seek Professional Help if Needed**: If family issues are deeply rooted and difficult to resolve, consider seeking the help of a family therapist or counselor.

Remember that building better family relationships is a continual process that requires effort from everyone involved. Be patient and understanding, and focus on fostering a loving and supportive environment within your family.

Take a minute to write down everything you want to *Be, Do*, and *Have* in your Family Spoke. Write your answers in the three columns below. Identify what you want in your family life and write it down. Here are some things that I wanted in my Family Spoke.

FAMILY SPOKE

BE	DO	Have
Available	Spend quality time	A solid connection
Truthful	Do what you say	Trust
Responsible	Put family needs first	Unity
Forgiving	Lose the grudge	A second chance
Happy	Have some fun	Better communication

Now, you do it.

BE	DO	Have

Now that you have written down the things you want to be, do, and have, how are you going to get them? What is the next step in building your plan for success? The "Be, Do, Have" list is general information. Now is the time to get specific. Ask yourself *why* you want to be, do, or have the things you listed. This exercise will eliminate the items that might be frivolous, leaving you with a more specific goal to accomplish.

I have all the following character traits on my **BE** list—I want to be trustworthy, honest, dependable, loving, and kindhearted. Assuming I currently am none of the above, what could I do to accomplish that goal? I almost answer my own question by looking at my **DO** list. Looking at that list, how am I supposed to help others? This is very general, so we need to be more specific in our approach to setting goals.

The following steps will allow your goal to become a reality. Take a look at the table below. This exercise will break down the process of how you will achieve success and accomplish the goals you set for yourself. Identify some areas that you would like to grow in your Family Spoke.

Ziglar's Goals Procedure Chart

Identify your goal	Spend Quality Time with Kids
Benefits from reaching this goal	Stronger bond with each of them, letting them know how much they mean to me
Obstacles to overcome	Discipline to make this a priority, time to dedicate specifically to them
Skills and knowledge needed	Caring compassion and leadership
Individuals, organizations to help you	Tammie can help me schedule things and participate with us
Plan of action	Make sure I attend every performance, every game, and every pig showing contest they have. Make sure I'm available for them after school if they need help with homework or need someone to talk to.
Completion date	Jan 1, 2006

Now it's your turn to write down some specific goals using this procedure.

Identify your goal	
Benefits from reaching this goal	
Obstacles to overcome	
Skills and knowledge needed	
Individuals, organizations to help you	
Plan of action	
Completion date	

Remember the qualifying questions? Make sure your goals meet this criterion and that you can answer "YES" to all the questions.

- Is this really my goal?
- Is my goal morally right and fair to everyone concerned?
- Is this consistent with my other goals?
- Can I emotionally commit myself to finishing the goal?
- Can I see myself reaching the goal?
- Does it meet the requirements of the basic eight?

If you've made it this far, you probably have a great family goal to set your sights on. Now, do the work. Let's take this approach with all the other Spokes in your Wheel of Life. Taking the time to do this exercise will give you a roadmap to follow. It's a lot easier to get where you're going when you have a plan to get there. This will also bring more balance to your life.

SPIRITUAL SPOKE

I don't know about you, but I think that when there is a separation between me and God, one of us walked away, and in this case (as is always the case), it was me. I was the guy who thought I could do it all on my own, so I pretty much abandoned God because I had failed him in so many ways. He had delivered me from my drug addiction, and then I started sinning in other areas like being unfaithful to my wife. I felt ashamed and wasn't too sure how I would recover from that in the eyes of the Lord.

Does he still like me? Will I go to heaven? I had all these questions that centered around how I could try to restore that relationship. I started by identifying the problem on my Wheel of Life. I wrote down what I wanted to be as a result of the goal, and my answer was: I wanted to be more like Christ. How do you accomplish that? I wrote down a goal to spend 30 minutes per day in the Word reading the Bible and understanding him. I wrote down another goal, I will find a church and attend every Sunday.
That's where it started.

In doing that, I realized a few things. The most important discovery was that I was forgiven. Redemption was one of the keys to my success in this area because it gave me a healthier self-image as well as a clean slate to start from. The Spoke grew that year as I became more

> Redemption was one of the keys to my success in this area because it gave me a healthier self-image as well as a clean slate to start from.

involved in ministry work and had my kids in the Awana program. I became the director of the Awana program before the end of the year.

One year, I decided to go on a men's retreat, and I brought one of my sons with me. We were able to either camp out in a tent that we brought, or we could share a room with some other guys we didn't know. Anyway, I figured it would be better to spend time with just my son and God, so we put up the tent. We were having a great time shooting guns and bows and arrows, then hiking over a bridge. At the end of the night, we went to the tent to get some sleep.

At about 4 a.m., it started to rain hard. Then the wind picked up and woke us. The tent was filling up with water and was about to blow over. The top of the tent was blown down on us, and we got out of our sleeping bags. I held the tent up with both hands, but the wind just draped it around me. Then it started to hail. I was getting hit by golf ball size hail on my hands as I held that tent in place over me and my son. I looked down, and he looked terrified. He said, "Dad, I'm scared!" Truth was, so was I. Mother nature does not mess around in Texas.

The hail pounded me for about 30 minutes. After a half hour of sheer terror, my son looked at me and said, "It stopped, let's get in the car!" When we got out of what was left of the tent, the first thing we saw was a giant oak tree that had fallen on a Suburban truck and smashed it. Luckily no one was inside. Then we saw our car covered in broken branches, leaves, and ice chunks. We ran for the car and got in and started it up. We were soaked and frozen.

The coolest thing about that experience happened right there in the car as I looked at my son and said, "I saw you grabbing my leg and looking at me with total fear in your eyes as I held that tent up."

He said, "Yeah it was scary."

I said, "Son, when the storms of life come, they come hard and fast. But you can always know that when you're scared, you can always look up and your father will protect you just like I did in the tent." Wow, talk about a memory. That one should have made an impact on my boy.

I still work on my Spiritual Spoke every day as I write a blog in Zig's honor on Facebook called "One Year Daily Insights." The page was built around one of Zig's books by the same name. It is a daily devotional that I have done since his passing over ten years ago. Being in the Word daily for all these years has strengthened my faith and helped me share my testimony to help others. Please go search for the page, I would love to have you there with us for daily fellowship and advice that can help your life run a little smoother.

> "Son, when the storms of life come, they come hard and fast. But you can always know that when you're scared, you can always look up and your father will protect you just like I did in the tent."

Spiritual growth helps you develop the character of a godly person, and that, my friends, will help you in more ways than one. But let's get real. Where are you on this Spoke? Are you a believer in Christ? Do you read his Word daily? Or is your life with God just sitting on a shelf waiting for you to break it out in times of distress? Will you have eternal life? What about this, remember I was talking about having a healthy self-image? What does God think about you? Once you know who you are in Christ and, more importantly, *whose* you are, you begin to see yourself differently, and you will want to share the good news with everyone. Rate yourself on this Spoke and write down some things you would like to see come to fruition in your spiritual life.

What if that drug addict chose to follow Jesus Christ and never did hard drugs again? That is my testimony. God forgives us for those times in our lives when we made mistakes and bad decisions, and he uses them

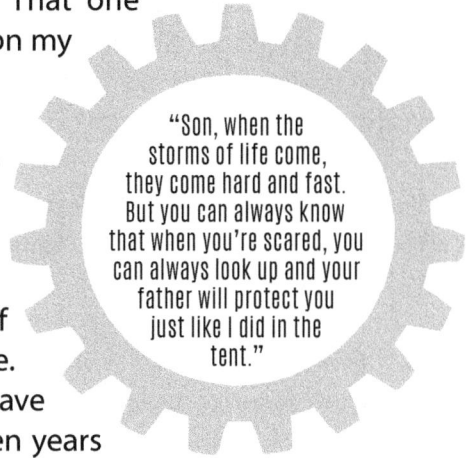

for his good purposes. Don't ever let your mistakes keep you from the one who can help you overcome them. God offers hope where there was none. You might say, "Well I don't go to church because they are a bunch of hypocrites." Don't let that stop you because there is plenty of room for one more. Besides that, if you're letting a hypocrite get in between you and God, the hypocrite is closer to God than you are. Here are a few things you can do to grow spiritually:

Growing spiritually is a deeply personal and enriching journey that can bring greater meaning and fulfillment to your life. Here are some practices and activities you can explore to foster spiritual growth:

1. **Meditation and Mindfulness**: Practice meditation or mindfulness to cultivate inner peace, focus, and self-awareness. These practices can help you connect with your inner self and develop a deeper understanding of your thoughts and emotions.
2. **Prayer and Reflection**: Engage in prayer or quiet reflection to connect with your beliefs, values, and higher power. This can provide a sense of guidance and purpose in life.
3. **Reading Sacred Texts**: Explore and study the Bible or spiritual literature relevant to your beliefs. These writings often contain wisdom and insights that can inspire personal growth.
4. **Practice Gratitude**: Develop a habit of expressing gratitude daily. Reflect on the positive aspects of your life and appreciate the blessings you have. We should always have an attitude of gratitude.
5. **Spend Time in Nature**: Connect with the natural world by spending time outdoors. Nature can be a source of peace, inspiration, and a reminder of the interconnectedness of all living beings.
6. **Engage in Acts of Kindness**: Practice compassion and kindness towards others. Engaging in acts of service can deepen your sense of purpose and interconnectedness with the world.

7. **Join a local Church**: Participate in a spiritual community or group that shares your beliefs and values. Engaging with like-minded individuals can provide support and foster spiritual growth.
8. **Practice Forgiveness**: Let go of grudges and practice forgiveness, both towards yourself and others. Forgiveness can lead to healing and emotional liberation.
9. **Explore Christianity**: Be open to learning about and understanding belief systems and spiritual traditions. Expanding your knowledge can enrich your own spiritual journey.
10. **Journaling**: Keep a spiritual journal to record your thoughts, reflections, and experiences. Writing can help clarify your thoughts and provide a record of your spiritual growth over time.
11. **Yoga or Tai Chi**: Engage in practices like yoga or Tai Chi, which combine physical movement with spiritual and meditative elements, promoting balance and inner harmony.
12. **Creative Expression**: Explore creative activities like art, music, or writing. Creative expression can be a powerful way to connect with your deeper self and explore your spirituality.
13. **Silent Retreats**: Consider participating in a silent retreat to disconnect from the noise of daily life and deepen your inner reflection and spiritual connection.

Remember that spiritual growth is a gradual process, and it's essential to be patient and compassionate with yourself. Find practices that resonate with you and create a balance that fits your lifestyle. The key is to be open-minded, curious, and willing to explore different paths on your spiritual journey.

Take a minute to write down everything you want to *Be, Do,* and *Have* in your Spiritual Spoke. Write your answers in the three columns below. This is step one in the goal setting process. Identify what you want in your life and write it down. Here are some things I wanted in my Spiritual Spoke.

SPIRITUAL SPOKE

BE	DO	Have
Trustworthy	Help others	Peace of mind
Honest	Read God's Word	Wisdom
Dependable	Go to church	Forgiveness
Loving	Start a ministry	Better relationships
Kindhearted	Share the Gospel	Eternal life

Now, you do it. Zig always said you have to **BE** the right kind of person and **DO** the right kind of things if you want to **HAVE** everything in life that you want. You will want to do this exercise with each one of the Spokes. There are no wrong answers here. Just list out what you want, that's step one to developing your plan.

BE	DO	Have

Now that you have written down the things you want to be, do, and have, how are you going to get them? Now is the time to get specific. Ask yourself *why* you want to be, do, or have the things you listed. This exercise will eliminate the items that might be frivolous, leaving you with a more specific goal to accomplish.

The following steps will allow your goal to become a reality. Take a look at the table below. This exercise will break down the process of how you will achieve success and accomplish the goals you set.

Ziglar's Goals Procedure Chart

Identify your goal	Start an online ministry
Benefits from reaching this goal	Helping others find answers and inspiring hope. I will learn the Scriptures by posting them daily.
Obstacles to overcome	Scheduling time to do it every day
Skills and knowledge needed	Communication skills and a daily devotional to follow would make this easier.
Individuals, organizations to help you	Michael Norton and Zig's book, *One Year Daily Insights* will help me get on track
Plan of action	Create Facebook page called One Year Daily Insights, invite friends and family to share the page. Post a scripture verse followed by what you would do to implement the biblical concept into your life. End with a prayer.
Completion date	Jan 1, 2013

Now it's your turn to write down some specific goals using this procedure.

Identify your goal	Start an online ministry
Benefits from reaching this goal	
Obstacles to overcome	
Skills and knowledge needed	
Individuals, organizations to help you	
Plan of action	
Completion date	

Remember the qualifying questions? Make sure your goals meet those criteria and that you can answer "YES" to all the questions.

- Is this really my goal?
- Is my goal morally right and fair to everyone concerned?
- Is this consistent with my other goals?
- Can I emotionally commit myself to finishing the goal?
- Can I see myself reaching the goal?
- Does it meet the requirements of the basic eight?

MENTAL SPOKE

It was a new year, 2007, and some new goals were set. This time, they were in the area of my education. I had really been wanting to go back to school and get my degree but just never really planned it out and set the goal. One day, one of my sons came to me and said, "Hey Dad, you make great money and dropped out of school, why do I need to go to college?

Wow, talk about surprised, I told him that the business climate has changed and having a degree would give him the competitive edge in the marketplace. He was just a freshman in high school at the time. Then he said something that made me really want to achieve this goal. He said, "Why don't you get your degree then?" Smart kid. I said, "You know what? I will have my bachelor's degree before you finish high school."

I sat down and wrote my goal to accomplish next. I found a school that was offering a degree in healthcare administration, and I went to school full time—while working full time and raising three children. Not an easy task. In fact it was probably the hardest goal I have ever set for myself.

It was strategic because at the time, Zig was not in very good health. He had fallen down a flight of stairs in his home, and it appeared that he had dementia. As things got real around the office, we were wondering how long Zig would be able to stay on the stage and do his motivational seminars. He was traveling all over the world to speak and then this accident happened. We all had to regroup for a while.

After some soul searching, I decided to leave Ziglar and pursue other opportunities in medical sales. My work experience was mostly in the radiology medical sales arena, so I decided to study Healthcare Administration to better understand my customers. I was able to land a job in the digital x-ray sales business, so the education piece was a very smart and timely move for me. More on that in the Career Spoke section later.

I worked on papers until midnight several days a week and on weekends too. I put everything I had, including $47,000, to pay for the education I was getting. I continued this for four years, working through summers and everything. I never took a break. On May 23, 2011, I took my last test, submitted my final paper, and graduated a week before my son did.

The dividends from going through that experience were huge. My son couldn't use me as an excuse to not go to school anymore. I accomplished another great goal for my life, and it was really helping me sell more equipment as I was able to see the transaction through the eyes of an administrator rather than just a sales guy. It gave me a better perspective on what was important to the people I was selling to and gave me a competitive edge as I was able to better understand their needs. This launched my career to new heights.

I also learned how to write during this period. My written and verbal skills were better because I picked up some new vocabulary and concepts that were relatable in my field of work. This goal helped me with all the other Spokes as well as I continued my journey on my *Wheel of Life*.

I have continued to come back to this Spoke to further develop my Mental Spoke. I went back to Ziglar's office and decided to get the Ziglar Legacy Certification. I am now a certified trainer and business coach, and some of the things I learned are in this book. Never stop learning new things.

Maybe the Mental spoke isn't about education for you. Maybe it's dealing with a trauma from your past. Maybe it's about forgiving someone who wronged you. Perhaps you struggle with anger, PTSD, anxiety or depression. I had to change my behavior and my mindset because I was struggling with all these things. Listen, going to therapy is a great mental goal if it helps you overcome a problem in your psyche. There is no judgement in doing everything in your power to change a bad behavior you might have clung to in order to cope with something.

There is no judgement in doing everything in your power to change a bad behavior you might have clung to in order to cope with something.

Another area I have continued to develop mentally is in the area of addiction.
Overcoming addiction is a challenging but achievable journey with the right approach and support. Here are some essential pieces of advice to help you on this path: If addiction is a chapter of your life, it doesn't have to be your entire book. Seek help from those who have dealt with it successfully and consider these ideas:

1. **Recognize the problem**: Acknowledging that you have an addiction is the first step towards recovery. Be honest with yourself and understand the negative impact it's having on your life and the lives of those around you.
2. **Seek professional help:** Addiction can be a complex issue, and professional support can make a significant difference. Reach out to a healthcare professional, counselor, therapist, or support group specialized in addiction treatment. They can provide personalized guidance and strategies to cope with withdrawal symptoms and triggers.
3. **Build a support network**: Surround yourself with understanding and supportive individuals who encourage your recovery efforts. This may include family, friends, support groups, or online communities. Sharing your

struggles with others who have faced similar challenges can be empowering and reassuring.

4. **Create a relapse prevention plan**: Identify triggers and situations that might lead to a relapse. Develop a plan to cope with these challenges, such as finding alternative activities, reaching out to your support network, or using relaxation techniques.

5. **Practice self-care**: Taking care of your physical and emotional well-being is crucial during recovery. Engage in regular exercise, eat a balanced diet, get enough sleep, and practice stress-reducing activities like meditation or yoga.

6. **Replace addiction with positive habits**: Fill the void left by the addiction with healthy and constructive activities. Find hobbies or interests that you enjoy and that provide a sense of fulfillment and purpose. Tom Ziglar says, "the fastest way to success is replacing bad habits with good habits.

7. **Set realistic goals**: Recovery is a process that takes time and effort. Set achievable short-term and long-term goals to track your progress and stay motivated.

8. **Avoid triggers**: Identify and avoid people, places, or situations that may trigger cravings or temptations. If certain environments are associated with your addiction, staying away from them can help minimize the risk of relapse.

9. **Be patient and compassionate with yourself**: Overcoming addiction is not a linear process, and setbacks can happen. Be kind to yourself and avoid self-blame. Celebrate your progress, no matter how small, and learn from any relapses to improve your coping strategies.

10. **Consider therapy:** Cognitive-behavioral therapy (CBT), motivational interviewing, and other evidence-based therapies can be effective in treating addiction. These approaches help you understand the underlying reasons for your addiction and develop healthier coping mechanisms.

Remember that overcoming addiction is a courageous and transformative journey. Celebrate each step you take towards recovery, and never hesitate to seek help when needed. Your commitment to change and growth is a testament to your strength and resilience.

Several types of therapy have been found to be effective in dealing with PTSD (Post-Traumatic Stress Disorder), depression, and anxiety. Here are some of the most common and evidence-based therapeutic approaches:

1. **Cognitive-Behavioral Therapy** (CBT): CBT is a widely used and effective therapy for PTSD, depression, and anxiety. It focuses on identifying and changing negative thought patterns and behaviors that contribute to emotional distress. CBT helps individuals learn healthier coping strategies and develop problem-solving skills.

2. **Eye Movement Desensitization and Reprocessing** (EMDR): This worked wonders for me. EMDR is specifically designed to address PTSD by processing traumatic memories and reducing their emotional impact. This therapy involves guided eye movements or other forms of bilateral stimulation while focusing on traumatic memories, helping to desensitize the distress associated with them.

3. **Acceptance and Commitment Therapy** (ACT): ACT is a mindfulness-based approach that aims to increase psychological flexibility and acceptance of distressing thoughts and emotions. It helps individuals focus on their values and take committed action toward a meaningful life despite their symptoms.

4. **Mindfulness-Based Therapies**: These therapies, such as Mindfulness-Based Cognitive Therapy (MBCT) and Mindfulness-Based Stress Reduction (MBSR), emphasize present-moment awareness and acceptance. They can be beneficial in managing anxiety and depression symptoms.

5. **Interpersonal Therapy** (IPT): IPT focuses on improving interpersonal relationships and communication to alleviate symptoms of depression. It helps individuals address

conflicts, loss, or life transitions that may be contributing to their emotional struggles.

6. **Dialectical Behavior Therapy** (DBT): DBT is commonly used to treat conditions like borderline personality disorder, but it can also be helpful for those with PTSD, depression, and anxiety. It combines cognitive-behavioral techniques with mindfulness practices to improve emotion regulation and interpersonal skills.

7. **Trauma-Focused Cognitive-Behavioral Therapy** (TF-CBT): Specifically designed for children and adolescents with PTSD, TF-CBT addresses trauma-related symptoms through cognitive and behavioral interventions, as well as family support.

8. **Group Therapy**: Group therapy can be beneficial for individuals dealing with PTSD, depression, or anxiety. Sharing experiences and emotions with others who have similar struggles can foster a sense of connection and support.

9. **Psychodynamic Therapy**: This therapy explores unconscious patterns and unresolved conflicts that may contribute to emotional difficulties. It can be helpful for individuals seeking a deeper understanding of their experiences and emotions.

It's essential to remember that therapy is not a one-size-fits-all approach. The effectiveness of each therapy may vary from person to person. A qualified mental health professional can help determine which type of therapy or combination of approaches is best suited for an individual's unique needs and circumstances.

You may not be an addict, a dropout or have a few mental issues like me, however, there is always something new to learn, so I encourage you to find opportunities to try new things and discover what you're capable of.

Take a minute to write down everything you want to Be, Do, and Have in your Mental Spoke.

MENTAL SPOKE

BE	DO	Have
Articulate	Write a journal	Better communication
Informed	Research	New knowledge
Teachable	Learn new things	Diversity
Engaging	Discuss ideas	Understanding
Educated	Finish degree	Marketability

Now you do it.

BE	DO	Have

Ziglar's Goals Procedure Chart

Identify your goal	Get my bachelor's in healthcare administration
Benefits from reaching this goal	Improved reading and writing skills I can use at work. My son not using my past failure as an excuse to not go to school.
Obstacles to overcome	Scheduling time to do it every day, having money to pay for it.
Skills and knowledge needed	Basic computer skills and an understanding of online classroom environment.
Individuals, organizations to help you	Tammie could help with kids so I can study and do homework.
Plan of action	Enroll in an online accredited university. Dedicate 3 hours per day during the week to study and do the work from 7-10 p.m. Do papers on weekends.
Completion date	April 2007-May 2011

Now it's your turn to write down some specific goals using this procedure.

Identify your goal	
Benefits from reaching this goal	
Obstacles to overcome	
Skills and knowledge needed	
Individuals, organizations to help you	
Plan of action	
Completion date	

Remember the qualifying questions? Make sure your goals meet this criterion and that you can answer "YES" to all the questions.

CAREER SPOKE

When life gets hard, we have a choice to either get bitter or get better. My desire is to take all that I have learned from Ziglar and inspire people with hope, help them achieve their dreams, and become all that God has created them to become.

As I said earlier, toward the end of my time with the Ziglar corporation, I knew things were about to change due to Zig's condition. Around that time, a guy came to my house to sell me life insurance. After hearing me talk about Zig and everything that was going on, he said, "I have a friend you need to talk to. He owns a company that sells digital x-ray solutions, and he is looking for a sales guy right now. You would be a perfect fit."

I took him up on it and met with the gentleman who owned the company, Neil. After a nice meeting, he advised me that he had just hired a person for the job a few days before. I asked him, "What if I were to take a segment nobody is working right now and do it on commission only?"

He said, "What did you have in mind?"

I said, "The oil and gas industry."

He laughed and said, "Go for it, we operate our equipment in cruise ships all over the world, so if you can sell medical equipment to oil and gas companies, you won't be running into anyone there because I'm not sure there is any business to be had." I shook his hand, and we agreed on a commission plan.

That conversation took place around lunchtime but by 3 p.m., I was on the phone with the medical director of all healthcare worldwide for ExxonMobil company. I called Neil and said, "I have Dr. Richard Dockins with ExxonMobil company on the line, and he needs two digital x-ray systems in Nigeria. Can we bring the unit to Houston to show it to him?" Neil's answer was, Yes, we can; and yes, I closed a $550,000 sale. I then got to travel to Nigeria as part of the deal, and it was an amazing experience to say the least. Not too long after that, I replaced the sales guy they had hired right before I came along.

I began to hone my selling skills and discipline myself to really charge hard. My next sale was a $880,000 job for a spinal clinic in San Antonio. I really learned a lot from a guy there named Kevin Borden. He was a technical service guy who really understood digital x-ray a lot better than I did, so we hit the road together a lot. We took a trip to Venice, Italy to install some equipment on a new Carnival cruise ship out there. We had a great time and developed a lifelong friendship as our combined efforts always seemed to produce a positive outcome. We remain the best of friends to this day even though we no longer work with each other. There is a saying, "If you see a turtle on top of a fence post, you know he must have gotten some help getting up there".

In 2008, I took a job with a larger dealer, Southwest X-ray Company, and stayed there for almost ten years. I worked for a man named Neal Shuefler—a sales giant. He was the most unorthodox salesperson I have ever met, but the guy really knew his stuff, and he sold a lot of x-ray gear. One huge lesson I learned from Neal was that the customer is hiring us to do a job because we know what we're doing. We are the ones who understand the x-ray capabilities better than anyone. We are the experts, so we can use that to guide our customers to the right solution. He taught me to ask lots of questions so I could better understand the customer's needs.

One day I was in Chicago at a trade show, and I met Rusty Peyton, the owner of an x-ray manufacturing company, who was displaying his products at the show. We had a really great conversation. He wanted to know about Zig because he was a huge Ziglar fan, and often listened to those sales' strategy tapes in his car while he was out on the road. Long story short, I told him some funny stories, and we immediately had a great connection. About a week after the show, Rusty asked me to come build the western regional sales channel for his company. The territory comprised everything west of the Mississippi River, and there was almost no business in the area as they were based more in the east. I accepted the challenge.

As part of my Career Spoke goals, I decided to meet with every x-ray dealer in my territory in person. I embarked on a trip that started January 2, just one day after I had set the goal. Over the next five weeks, I covered more than 6000 miles and met with more than 30 dealers. When I returned, I had some new dealers and some revenue coming in. I have continued to set goals for my career, and it has led me to a nice place. After four years of ground pounding and putting in the work, I developed a $4,000,000 per year growth in my territory.

I am a contributing factor of one of the fastest growing companies in our market segment because I created an action plan then did the work. I'm still building that business today and can't believe the results that have come from having a plan and maintaining the discipline to stay on top of it. Obviously, having this kind of career growth affected my other Spokes as well. I became closer to God and trusted in him, I became a better dad because I was able to work from home and be there every day when my kids came home from school. It helped my marriage too because I had more time to spend with my wife.

The truth is, I believe I've been called to write this book in order to help as many people as I can. Zig's famous philosophy, "You can have everything in life that you want, if you just help enough other people get what they want," seems to be the focus on this book. I hope it helps everyone who decides to read it and implement the wheel of life into their own lives.

Growing your career requires careful planning, dedication, and continuous improvement. Here are some essential things to consider to help you navigate your career growth successfully:

1. **Set Clear Goals**: Define your short-term and long-term career goals. Knowing where you want to go will help you plan the necessary steps to get there.
2. **Continuous Learning**: Stay open to learning new skills and gaining knowledge relevant to your industry. Attend workshops, seminars, webinars, or pursue additional education if needed.
3. **Networking**: Build and maintain professional relationships within your industry. Networking can lead to valuable opportunities, collaborations, and insights.
4. **Seek Feedback**: Be open to feedback from colleagues, supervisors, or mentors. Constructive criticism can help you identify areas for improvement and accelerate your growth.
5. **Embrace Challenges**: Don't shy away from challenges or new responsibilities. Embracing opportunities to stretch yourself will help you develop and demonstrate your capabilities.
6. **Adaptability**: Be adaptable in the face of change and uncertainty. The job market and industries evolve, so being flexible and open to change is crucial for staying relevant.
7. **Personal Branding**: Cultivate a strong personal brand that showcases your skills, accomplishments, and unique qualities. Online platforms like LinkedIn can be powerful tools for personal branding.
8. **Work Ethic**: Demonstrate a strong work ethic by being reliable, punctual, and committed to producing quality work. Your dedication will be noticed and appreciated.
9. **Mentorship**: Seek out mentors who can offer guidance, support, and wisdom based on their experiences. A mentor can provide valuable insights into your career journey.

10. **Take Risks**: Calculated risks can lead to significant rewards in your career. Be willing to step outside your comfort zone and seize opportunities that align with your goals.
11. **Balance Work and Life**: Strive for a healthy work-life balance. Burnout can hinder your progress, so take time for self-care, hobbies, and spending time with loved ones.
12. **Stay Positive and Resilient**: Facing setbacks and challenges is normal in any career. Stay positive, maintain resilience, and learn from any obstacles you encounter.
13. **Track Your Achievements**: Keep a record of your accomplishments and contributions. This can be helpful when updating your resume or during performance evaluations.
14. **Stay Informed About Industry Trends**: Be aware of the latest trends and developments in your field. Staying informed positions you as someone who is forward-thinking and up-to-date.
15. **Advocate for Yourself**: Don't be afraid to advocate for your career growth. If you believe you deserve a promotion or a raise, communicate your achievements and contributions to your superiors.

> Calculated risks can lead to significant rewards in your career. Be willing to step outside your comfort zone and seize opportunities that align with your goals.

Remember that career growth is a continuous journey. It's okay to take detours and adjust your plans along the way. Be proactive, stay focused, and keep a growth mindset as you work towards building a successful and fulfilling career.

What are some areas you should focus on to help advance your career? In my case, advancing my Career Spoke helped drive my Financial Spoke. I'm in sales, so most of my goals were based around how I could grow that business.

Take a minute to write down everything you want to Be, Do, and Have in your Career Spoke.

CAREER SPOKE

BE	DO	Have
Curious	Ask more questions	Better understanding
Tenacious	Go the extra mile	Increased pipeline
Relevant	Listen to understand	Better solutions
Intelligent	Know your product	Confidence
Truthful	Be real	Integrity

Now you do it.

BE	DO	Have

Ziglar's Goals Procedure Chart

Identify your goal	Get Ziglar Legacy Certification
Benefits from reaching this goal	After looking at my BE, DO, HAVE list, most of those character traits are taught in the classes. Increased communication skills could get me better sales results. The motivation aspects could help me go further.
Obstacles to overcome	Getting time off work to go. Having the money for the training.
Skills and knowledge needed	Come with an open mind and take lots of notes
Individuals, organizations to help you	Tom Ziglar, Laurie Magers
Plan of action	Go to Dallas to attend the ZLC Conference in May. Learn new skills by getting certified in Tom's new *Choose to Win* class as well as Presentation skills.
Completion date	May 2018

Now it's your turn to write down some specific goals using this procedure.

Identify your goal	
Benefits from reaching this goal	
Obstacles to overcome	
Skills and knowledge needed	
Individuals, organizations to help you	
Plan of action	
Completion date	

Remember the qualifying questions? Make sure your goals meet this criterion and that you can answer "YES" to all the questions.

FINANCIAL SPOKE

To review: I had lost my company, the bank foreclosed on my house and took my car, and I had to file for bankruptcy. I had nothing left to my name. I started over, and by the time I decided to focus on my Financial Spoke, I was making good money. But I was not really investing it in anything. I had gone from being young and broke, to having great money, back to being totally broke. This time I was a little smarter. I saved my money instead of spending all of it. The only money you will ever have is the money you save and invest.

I recommend everyone pays themselves something and that money should go into an account for what you want down the road. I had purchased a house and everything else I paid for in cash. I had an old Honda Accord I paid cash for, and I drove that thing until I had enough money saved up to buy a better car. I never had credit card debt after bankruptcy because I couldn't get a credit card. My credit score was terrible at 550, so I just kept saving.

I remember telling myself *when I get $5,000 in my savings, I'm going to act like that is my zero balance.* So, I would not ever go below that number. I saved another $5000. Then I told myself $10,000 was my zero balance, and I didn't go below that. This trend continued as I tried to save every penny. One day I closed a deal worth $880,000, and my commission was over $40,000. I took what was left after getting robbed by the taxes on it and was able to purchase 2.5 acres of land on Canyon Lake that was foreclosing for $24,000. This was my first investment property.

As my career started to take off and the sales were coming in, I kept saving. One day I finally got to a point where my "zero balance" was $50,000 in the savings account. I can't tell you the freedom that comes with not having debt and having a nice cushion in the bank in case something happens. It brings you confidence and stability, and that carries back to your attitude and performance in all these other areas of life.

I really wanted to move, but for whatever reason I just could not find a buyer for the house I was living in. So I decided to do a little work on the lake property and see if I could sell it. I hired a guy to clear out some cedar trees from the top acre. He only charged me $1,500 to do the work, and it really opened up the view of the Twin Sisters Peaks in the background. Now a prospective buyer could see the beautiful view they would have from their backyard.

There is something pretty amazing in this story that I want to talk about. You see, my wife and I tried to sell that house three times, and it showed well every time, but we had no buyers. We found homes we loved, and we put contingent offers on them, but we lost out because we couldn't sell our existing home. We were discouraged and outraged because of it. I couldn't figure out why we couldn't sell that place. We were constantly keeping it cleaned up and ready to show. If you have ever had to sell a house, you know what I'm talking about. It is a challenge, with three kids at home, to keep a place "show ready."

After listing it three times and not getting any bites, we found our dream home which happened to be a lot nicer than the previous "dream homes." Better location and better layout. It couldn't be any better for us. So, we decided to sell the property for the down payment rather than selling the house we were currently living in so we could rent that house. It worked great.

I sold the land for $69,000, and we moved into our new home. Now we had an income stream from the rental, so we just kept saving money and buying more rent houses. Today, I own four houses and am so proud of how I have used my finances. If I had just kept borrowing like I did the first time around, rather than saving every penny, I would never be in this good of a situation. Even better, here in my area of Texas, the value of those properties has almost doubled in the past five years.

I want you to hear this. Our plans kept failing—we couldn't sell the house—but God's plans were better. Sometimes we try to force something to happen, and we struggle and fight through a season of difficulty only to find out that our way was nowhere near as cool as God's way. Be patient, don't stress, because when something doesn't work out, maybe it's because something better is on its way.

Use your money as a vehicle that generates more money. Whether you invest in real estate, 401k, IRA, Crypto, gold, whatever your vehicle is, use it to make more money. When you spend all your money and then borrow more from the bank at terrible interest rates, it just buries you, leaving you in a hole that you can't dig yourself out of.

> Sometimes we try to force something to happen, and we struggle and fight through a season of difficulty only to find out that our way was nowhere near as cool as God's way. Be patient, don't stress, because when something doesn't work out, maybe it's because something better is on its way.

Like Dave Ramsey says, pay off your debt, then save your money. Start with the smallest debt, knock it out, and go to the next one, until all your stuff is paid for. Have a cushion in savings in case some emergency happens, or someone loses a job. Put at least six months' worth of living expenses in your account and call it *zero*. This will bring the stress level at home down a few notches.

Zig always said, "Money isn't everything, but it is reasonably close to oxygen. I love all the things money can buy, but I love the things money can't buy better. Money can buy you a bed but not a good night's sleep, a house but not a home, a companion but not a friend." Get disciplined with your spending and use your resources on investments that will bring you a good return.

Great financial goals are specific, achievable, and aligned with your overall financial plan. They vary based on individual circumstances and priorities, but here are some common and important financial goals to consider:

1. **Emergency Fund**: Build an emergency fund that covers 3 to 6 months' worth of living expenses. This fund acts as a safety net in case of unexpected events like medical emergencies, job loss, or major repairs.
2. **Debt Repayment**: Set a goal to pay off high-interest debts, such as credit card balances or personal loans. Being debt-free reduces financial stress and frees up money for other purposes.
3. **Retirement Savings**: Plan for your retirement by contributing regularly to retirement accounts like 401(k)s or IRAs. Aim to maximize your contributions to take advantage of employer matches or tax benefits.
4. **Education Savings**: If you have children or plan to pursue further education, consider setting up a college savings fund, such as a 529 plan, to help cover education expenses.
5. **Down Payment for a Home**: If homeownership is a goal, start saving for a down payment on a house. A larger down payment can lead to lower monthly mortgage payments and better loan terms.
6. **Investing**: Develop an investment strategy aligned with your risk tolerance and financial goals. Investing can help your money grow over time and build wealth.
7. **Multiple Income Streams**: Aim to diversify your income sources to increase financial security. This could include side gigs, freelancing, rental properties, or investing in dividend-paying stocks.

8. **Travel and Experiences**: Set aside funds for travel and experiences that enrich your life. Experiences can be more fulfilling than material possessions and create lasting memories.
9. **Charitable Giving**: Plan to give back to your community or support causes that are important to you. Charitable giving can provide a sense of fulfillment and help those in need.
10. **Savings for Major Purchases**: Whether it's a new car, home renovations, or other significant expenses, having a savings goal for major purchases can prevent you from going into debt.
11. **Healthcare and Insurance**: Prioritize health and insurance needs. Regularly review your health insurance coverage and consider adding life, disability, or long-term care insurance to protect your family's financial well-being.
12. **Career Development**: Invest in your professional development to enhance your earning potential. This could include further education, certifications, or attending workshops and conferences.
13. **Estate Planning**: Ensure that you have a will and other essential estate planning documents in place to protect your assets and provide for your loved ones in the event of your passing.

Remember, the key to achieving financial goals is to create a realistic budget, track your progress regularly, and make adjustments as needed. Financial goals should be flexible and adaptable to changes in your life and circumstances.

Living this way might mean giving up some things you enjoy in the short term. For example, cut down on going out to eat. After doing the reconciliation of my account, I found that eating out was my number one spending item. No more Starbucks, no more clubbing and drinking, and, in the long run, you will be able to do so much more. Start right away. Don't go another day without doing something for yourself in this Spoke.

Take a minute to write down everything you want to Be, Do, and Have in your Financial Spoke.

FINANCIAL SPOKE

BE	DO	Have
Frugal	Don't waste money	Something in savings
Consistent	Pay yourself every paycheck	Discipline
Aware	Pay attention to spending	Stay on top of it
Smart	Invest in real estate	Residual income
Grateful	Appreciate what you have	Appreciation

Now you do it.

BE	DO	Have

Ziglar's Goals Procedure Chart

Identify your goal	Save $5,000
Benefits from reaching this goal	Have a little safety net in the bank in case something happens.
Obstacles to overcome	Discipline to save and not blow my money.
Skills and knowledge needed	Financial advice
Individuals, organizations to help you	Read Dave Ramsey's book *Total Money Makeover* and adapt some of his principles into my program
Plan of action	First, make a few changes like not eating out as much and watch spending. Second, make it a priority to pay myself back 15% of all my income for future use.
Completion date	Jan 1, 2008

Now it's your turn to write down some specific goals using this procedure.

Identify your goal	
Benefits from reaching this goal	
Obstacles to overcome	
Skills and knowledge needed	
Individuals, organizations to help you	
Plan of action	
Completion date	

Remember the qualifying questions? Make sure your goals meet this criterion and that you can answer "YES" to all the questions.

PHYSICAL SPOKE

What if the kid who was always getting picked on chose to join the Army and grew strong enough that no one ever picked on him again? That was a nice change that happened to me, but as the years went by, my weight kept going up. I had all this success in all these areas of my life, but I looked like a tugboat. I was 80 pounds overweight and felt miserable about myself.

Here I had the solution the entire time, but I put my own health at the back of the line, and it was showing up on my waistline. I weighed in at 257 pounds one day and decided to write down some goals in this area of my life.

I got started and did a deal called Optavia for about 90 days, and I lost 60 pounds. The diet consisted of five "fueling's" and one healthy meal per day. No carbs, no processed foods, no sodas, no alcohol, no cheat meals. Just fuelings, lean protein and veggies once a day, and all I drank was water and black coffee. It was the most boring 90 days of my life, but I felt great because I was able to get rid of 60 pounds of lard from my gut.

I honestly was able to go out and purchase new clothes. I remember going to Men's Warehouse and buying a couple of new suits. The cool thing was I found one that fit right. I cannot explain the frustration that takes place when you wear a size 50 jacket and a 38" waist. If you've got a big gut, you can't find a suit. You have to piece something together, and it usually doesn't look so great. It was awesome to see myself with all that confidence looking back at me in the mirror.

I showed up to the RSNA in Chicago, and the people I work with were totally blown away. I was under 200 pounds for the first time in a decade, and it felt great. Unfortunately, I went back to the old lifestyle of eating garbage and drinking booze. About a year later, I was back up to 230 pounds, and my clothes were stretched to the max.

It was clear I needed to do something to regain control. This time I had a better understanding of nutrition and what worked for me diet-wise, but I wanted to incorporate exercise this time so the weight might stay off for a while. I was online one day and saw that a friend of mine was doing the "75 Hard Challenge."

In 2020, Andy Frisella came out with a book called *75 Hard*, and it is pretty hard to accomplish unless you have the mindset and the goals written down every day. I got serious and decided I was going to do the challenge. It requires you to do two 45-minute workouts per day, one of those workouts must be done outdoors in the elements. I actually did both of my workouts outside most days. Rain or shine, hot or cold, it didn't matter. I had to go do it, and I did it twice a day, every day.

I also had to follow a diet, so I did what I was doing before, except I ate a couple meals a day instead of just one. Always meat and veggies and those Optavia feulings in between meals. None of the bad stuff. I had to drink one gallon of water per day, every day. I had to read ten pages from a book that was teaching me a new skill every day. I had to report and take a picture of my progress every day as well.

Seventy-five days later, I was back under 200 pounds, but this time I felt strong. I had been able to integrate so many good habits into my life that I now know that if I start to gain weight, I just get back after it to keep myself in check. I tend to go up and down with my weight because old habits are hard to break, and let's face it, beer goes great with pizza.

First thing you will notice when you lose a ton of weight is everyone will compliment you. I am not a shy person, but I must admit, the attention was more than I expected. Many people will rally behind your efforts to help you achieve success if you bring them into it. I would post results daily and get so much encouragement that I couldn't stop. Once I started this, I had everyone in my circle of influence cheering for me. It was awesome.

Nothing can replace the feeling of accomplishment, confidence, and pride that completing something like this brings you. If you are struggling with your weight, maybe you should write down some goals and try to get in better shape. What would you want to Be, Do, or Have in the Physical Spoke? Would you want to lose weight? Be more athletic? Be able to run again? Then make yourself a priority, because if you don't, you will not be able to enjoy all the other great things you've done and will do in your life. What good is it to have a pile of money if you're lying in bed sick?

> ..make yourself a priority, because if you don't, you will not be able to enjoy all the other great things you've done and will do in your life.

Think about the changes you can make right now that would improve your health. Are you moving? Exercise is vital. Get to drinking some water on a regular basis. We often feel hungry when we are really just thirsty. Drink a gallon a day. Eat good whole foods not the processed garbage you find in a box. The food that God created for us to eat will always bring you more nutritional value than the man-made foods. Change those bad habits into good habits and I guarantee you will be not only growing the Physical Spoke but it will have an affect on the other spokes as well.

Improving your physical health is essential for overall well-being and a higher quality of life. Here are some actionable steps you can take to enhance your physical health:

1. **Regular Exercise**: Engage in regular physical activity that you enjoy, such as walking, jogging, swimming, cycling, or dancing. Aim for at least 150 minutes of moderate-intensity exercise or 75 minutes of vigorous-intensity exercise per week, as recommended by health guidelines.

2. **Strength Training**: Incorporate strength training exercises into your routine. It helps build muscle, improves metabolism, and enhances bone density. You can use bodyweight exercises or work with resistance bands, dumbbells, or weight machines.

3. **Balanced Diet**: Adopt a balanced and nutritious diet rich in fruits, vegetables, whole grains, lean proteins, and healthy fats. Limit processed foods, sugary drinks, and excessive sodium and saturated fats.

4. **Stay Hydrated**: Drink plenty of water throughout the day to maintain hydration and support bodily functions.

5. **Adequate Sleep**: Prioritize getting 7-9 hours of quality sleep each night. Sleep is crucial for physical and mental recovery and overall health.

6. **Manage Stress**: Find healthy ways to manage stress, such as mindfulness, meditation, yoga, or spending time in nature. Chronic stress can have negative effects on your physical health.

7. **Limit Alcohol and Avoid Smoking**: If you drink alcohol, do so in moderation, and avoid smoking or any tobacco products altogether.

8. **Regular Check-ups**: Schedule regular medical check-ups and screenings with your healthcare provider to monitor your health and catch any potential issues early.

9. **Practice Good Hygiene**: Wash your hands frequently, especially during flu seasons, and practice good hygiene habits to reduce the risk of infections.

10. **Maintain a Healthy Weight**: Strive to maintain a healthy weight that is appropriate for your age, height, and body type. If needed, work with a healthcare professional to develop a safe and sustainable weight management plan.

11. **Sun Protection**: Protect your skin from harmful UV rays by wearing sunscreen, sunglasses, and protective clothing when exposed to the sun.
12. **Limit Sedentary Time**: Reduce the time spent sitting or being sedentary by taking breaks and incorporating movement throughout your day.
13. **Social Connections**: Maintain healthy social connections with friends, family, and community members. Social interactions contribute to overall well-being.
14. **Stay Informed About Health Issues**: Stay informed about health-related topics and follow health guidelines to make informed decisions about your well-being.
15. **Be Patient and Consistent**: Improving physical health is a journey that requires patience and consistency. Set realistic goals and celebrate your progress along the way.

Remember that small changes can add up to significant improvements in your physical health. Choose one or two areas to focus on initially and gradually incorporate additional habits as you feel comfortable. Always consult with a healthcare professional before making significant changes to your diet or exercise routine, especially if you have any underlying health conditions.

Take a minute to write down everything you want to Be, Do, and Have in your Physical Spoke.

PHYSICAL SPOKE

BE	DO	Have
Disciplined	The work	Strength
Satisfied	Eat right	Energy
Confident	Positive self talk	Dignity
Strong	Push yourself	Resilience
Bold	Try something new	Satisfaction

Now you do it.

BE	DO	Have

Ziglar's Goals Procedure Chart

Identify your goal	Lose 30 lbs.
Benefits from reaching this goal	Happier, healthier self-image, clothes fitting better.
Obstacles to overcome	Dedicating the time to work out and meal prep
Skills and knowledge needed	Follow a program that incorporates an all-encompassing approach.
Individuals, organizations to help you	Read Andy Frisella's *75 Hard* and implement it into my day.
Plan of action	Do two 45-minute workouts every day, follow keto diet plan, drink one gallon of water every day. Read 10 pages from a book that will teach me something new every day. Take a daily progress picture.
Completion date	June 8, 2022

Now it's your turn to write down some specific goals using this procedure.

Identify your goal	
Benefits from reaching this goal	
Obstacles to overcome	
Skills and knowledge needed	
Individuals, organizations to help you	
Plan of action	
Completion date	

Remember the qualifying questions? Make sure your goals meet this criterion and that you can answer "YES" to all the questions.

PERSONAL SPOKE

This is a great Spoke because almost anything goes in here. What else do you want? Most of the things in this Spoke are for fun. I like being able to go on vacation, but this was a challenge for me for a few years after my bankruptcy as I had no money. One of the goals my wife and I have accomplished together is being able to go on a cruise or a trip once a year for our anniversary. We set back a small portion of our savings specifically for going on vacation to celebrate our marriage.

Generally speaking, when you allow yourself the opportunity to go on vacation and really get away from your daily routine to get some rest, you will always come back fired up and ready to get going in high gear when you return to work. You need down time so you can regroup and relax a little bit. In the long run, you won't feel burnt out. Studies show that when you get adequate rest, you perform better, have more stamina, and are more productive.

One of the recent goals I outlined in my personal goals procedure chart for this Spoke was building a woodshop in my backyard (see below). This goal was a project that started on a piece of scratch paper. I was able to design and be the general contractor as well as the project manager. When you take on new goals in your Personal Spoke, get ready to learn a bunch of new things. I found the tradesmen I needed and put them to work on my design.

It took about three months to complete the task. I had a guy come in and lay the concrete foundation, then a framer built the structure.

The same guy ended up doing the roofing and some of the finish work. A stucco guy did the exterior and paint, then an Insulation crew blew the foam. After that, my wife and I did most of the sheetrock and tongue and groove wood on the walls. We did all the taping and bedding of the sheetrock then textured it and painted the interior. I also did all the electrical and lighting myself, which saved some money.

Building the shop and attached "She Shed" gave us a place to put all our lawn and garden stuff. The space, which we call "ToeJam Workshop," is awesome because I can get my tools in a spot where the dust doesn't cover my cars. So, you are probably asking yourself, why do we call it ToeJam? It comes from a combination of our names: Joe and Tammie, Toe and Jammie—ToeJam. It's the dynamic duo nickname we gave ourselves. Team ToeJam has accomplished so many things in the 16 years we've been married. That woman is everything to me. My inspiration, my pride, my joy, my partner. I could not have accomplished any of these goals if it weren't for her standing by my side and encouraging me to keep going. I love you, Babe.

The new workshop gives me a space to create things. I love woodworking, and I make some unique pieces like brisket boards, cheese boards, tables, epoxy resin pieces, and so many other cool things. Having a place to create, to get away and express your talent or learn a new skill is a much better way to spend your free time than sitting in front of a TV screen. I use my creativity to make a project, then I usually give it to someone. People enjoy when you create gifts for them. It shows the person that they are worth your time and that you genuinely care about them. I make things for my customers, and they are always blown away when they receive that kind of a gift.

Finally, I want to talk about writing this book. I wanted to tell my story so I could help others the way people helped me. The truth is we learn more from teaching others than we do through any other methods. Hearing something gives you partial retention of the material. Reading things gives you a little more retention. Seeing things works better than that, but teaching something requires you to retain the information completely.

> The truth is we learn more from teaching others than we do through any other methods.

When I did Optavia, I was a coach. I helped other people lose weight while I was losing mine. This effort produced more interest on my part to really understand what I was doing. When I started doing the One Year Daily Insights page, I had the same outcome. If I had to share a daily message on Facebook, I was going to have to dive in and really be dedicated to understanding God's Word. In order to have a better understanding of the goal setting and achieving process, I started teaching goal setting and am now teaching you.

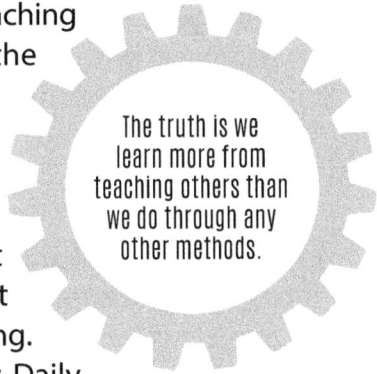

Developing yourself personally is an ongoing journey of self-discovery and growth. Here are some effective ways to nurture personal development:

1. **Set Clear Goals**: Define specific and achievable personal goals that align with your values and aspirations. Having clear objectives will guide your actions and focus your efforts.
2. **Continuous Learning**: Cultivate a love for learning by exploring new subjects, skills, or hobbies. Read books, take online courses, attend workshops, or listen to podcasts that expand your knowledge.
3. **Practice Self-Reflection**: Take time to reflect on your thoughts, emotions, and experiences. Self-reflection enhances self-awareness and helps identify areas for improvement.
4. **Embrace Change and Challenges**: Embrace change as an opportunity for growth and view challenges as learning experiences. Step out of your comfort zone and embrace new opportunities.

5. **Develop Emotional Intelligence**: Work on understanding and managing your emotions effectively. Emotional intelligence helps with self-regulation and building healthy relationships.

6. **Cultivate Positive Habits**: Adopt positive habits that contribute to your well-being, such as regular exercise, healthy eating, good sleep hygiene, and mindfulness practices.

7. **Practice Gratitude**: Cultivate a sense of gratitude by regularly acknowledging and appreciating the positive aspects of your life.

8. **Stay Curious**: Approach life with curiosity and an open mind. Stay curious about the world around you and actively seek to learn new things.

9. **Seek Feedback**: Be open to feedback from others, whether it's from friends, family, or colleagues. Constructive feedback can help you identify blind spots and areas for improvement.

10. **Surround Yourself with Positive Influences**: Surround yourself with people who inspire and support your personal growth. Seek out mentors or role models who can provide guidance.

11. **Keep a Journal**: Maintain a journal to record your thoughts, experiences, and personal growth journey. Writing can help clarify your thoughts and track your progress.

12. **Practice Mindfulness**: Engage in mindfulness practices to stay present and aware of your thoughts and actions. Mindfulness can reduce stress and improve focus.

13. **Set Healthy Boundaries**: Learn to set boundaries with others to protect your well-being and ensure a healthy balance in your relationships.

14. **Volunteer and Give Back**: Engaging in community service or volunteering can foster a sense of purpose and fulfillment.

15. **Celebrate Achievements**: Celebrate your accomplishments, no matter how small. Recognizing your successes boosts self-confidence and motivates further growth.

Remember that personal development is a lifelong process, and it's okay to take one step at a time. Be patient and compassionate with yourself as you navigate your journey of self-improvement. Celebrate the progress you make, and always strive to become the best version of yourself.

These were all Personal Spoke goals for me, and my life is so much more balanced and successful now that I've incorporated these teachings into my life.

Remember that personal development is a lifelong process, and it's okay to take one step at a time.

Take a minute to write down everything you want to Be, Do, and Have in your Personal Spoke.

PERSONAL SPOKE

BE	DO	Have
Adventurous	Travel	Fun
At peace	Relax	Rest
Creative	Build a shop	A place to create
Developing	New projects/rentals	Residual income
A teacher	Write a book	A Legacy

Now you do it.

BE	DO	Have

Ziglar's Goals Procedure Chart

Identify your goal	Build a woodshop in the backyard
Benefits from reaching this goal	A place to keep all my tools where I can keep the sawdust off my cars
Obstacles to overcome	Finding contractors, getting permits
Skills and knowledge needed	General construction and materials costs
Individuals, organizations to help you	Framer, Concrete guy, Stucco guy, Roofer
Plan of action	Design a woodshop, have a plan, get contractors to bid, select contract help. Procure the building materials. Manage project schedule and budget.
Completion date	June 2022

Now it's your turn to write down some specific goals using this procedure.

Identify your goal	
Benefits from reaching this goal	
Obstacles to overcome	
Skills and knowledge needed	
Individuals, organizations to help you	
Plan of action	
Completion date	

Remember the qualifying questions? Make sure your goals meet this criterion and that you can answer "YES" to all the questions.

CONCLUSION

In conclusion, I'm going to leave you with a few parting thoughts of wisdom. The reason I told my story was because I wanted to show the world that if some poor, high school drop out with a drug addiction can make it to the top, so can you. Give it your all. Create your roadmap to success and follow it to the letter. You will be accomplishing new things in no time.

Setting goals offers numerous advantages and benefits that can positively impact various aspects of your life. Here are some of the key advantages of setting goals:

1. **Clarity and Focus**: Goals provide clarity about what you want to achieve and help you stay focused on your priorities. They act as a roadmap, guiding your actions and decisions towards your desired outcomes.
2. **Motivation and Commitment**: Goals create a sense of purpose and motivation. When you have clear objectives, you're more likely to stay committed and take the necessary steps to achieve them.
3. **Measurable Progress**: Setting specific and measurable goals allows you to track your progress. Seeing your advancement over time can boost your confidence and encourage you to keep going.
4. **Time Management**: Goals help you manage your time efficiently. You can allocate your time and resources to tasks that align with your objectives, reducing distractions and increasing productivity.

5. **Overcoming Procrastination**: Having well-defined goals minimizes procrastination. Knowing what needs to be accomplished and when helps you avoid putting things off.

6. **Increased Accountability**: Goals hold you accountable for your actions. When you set goals, you take ownership of your journey and are more likely to take responsibility for your progress.

7. **Personal Growth**: Pursuing goals often involves stepping out of your comfort zone, which promotes personal growth and development. You acquire new skills and gain valuable experiences along the way.

8. **Decision Making**: Goals serve as a filter for decision-making. When faced with choices, you can assess whether they align with your goals, making it easier to make informed decisions.

9. **Resilience and Perseverance**: Working towards goals may involve overcoming obstacles and setbacks. This process builds resilience and teaches you to persevere even in challenging times.

10. **Sense of Achievement**: Achieving goals provides a sense of accomplishment and satisfaction. Celebrating your successes reinforces a positive mindset and encourages further progress.

11. **Improved Self-Confidence**: As you achieve your goals, your self-confidence grows. Believing in your abilities and seeing the results of your efforts can boost self-esteem.

12. **Enhanced Focus on Priorities**: Setting goals helps you identify what truly matters to you and allows you to prioritize activities that align with your values and aspirations.

13. **Better Time and Resource Management**: Having clear goals allows you to allocate your time, energy, and resources more efficiently, avoiding wasting them on unproductive activities.

14. **Healthy Challenge and Growth**: Goals provide healthy challenges that push you beyond your comfort zone, fostering continuous growth and development.

15. **Happiness and Fulfillment**: Pursuing meaningful goals contributes to a sense of happiness and fulfillment in life, as you are actively working towards creating the life you desire.

In summary, setting goals empowers you to take control of your life, create a sense of purpose, and achieve your dreams. Whether in personal or professional spheres, goal-setting is a powerful tool for success and personal fulfillment.

Here is something to chew on. How you see yourself will have a direct bearing on your success. If you think you are a winner, you will win more often. If you think you're a loser, you will probably lose more often. I said this earlier in the book, Dr. Joyce Brothers said, "You cannot consistently perform in a manner that is inconsistent with the way you see yourself." Look in the mirror every day and speak positive affirmations to yourself. Convince yourself that you are unstoppable, and no one will be able to stop you.

I will say this, you have two ears and one mouth, if you use them proportionately, you will have more success in your business as well as in your relationships. Always try to listen to understand, and that will carry you far in your relationships with others.

I want to thank God for being patient with me and for guiding me down this road of life. A couple of scriptures that grace my walls at home are Philippians 4:13, *I can do all things through Christ who strengthens me*, and Jeremiah 29:11, *For I have plans for you, plans to give you hope and a future.*

John Maxwell said, "Hope in the future is power in the present." Hope may not be a strategy, as my boss Todd Danner would say, but it is fuel for accomplishment, and that fuel will help you achieve anything you put your mind to.

Zig used to say, "You can have everything in life that you want, if you would just help enough other people get what they want." There are so many people to thank because they were there to help me get where I am, so I created my own "Wall of Gratitude" in my office.

Here are the people on my wall of gratitude that I would like to thank for getting me to where I am. I would like to wholeheartedly thank the following people who have mentored me and helped me along the way.

I would like to thank my mom and dad for doing the best they could with the hand they were dealt. They put up with a lot from me, and I'm sure neither one of them thought I would turn out to be where I am in life, but I got here because they taught me how to work hard.

I want to thank my wife, Tammie, for being there right beside me through all of this growth. By the way, when you start to accomplish great things in your life, your spouse will often also get some goals and try to do things with you. Tammie got her master's degree while I was getting my bachelor's. She lost weight and worked out when I did, and now, she is working on her CPA while I'm writing this book. Good partners help encourage each other to Be, Do, and Have everything in life they want.

I want to thank my children for putting up with me and doing these goals on January 1 every year with me. I hope you guys know how much you mean to me.

I want to thank Bruce Hammond for being such an amazing person and for sharing Christ with me when I needed to hear it. I learned so much from this man, and he will always have a special place in my life.

I want to thank Mark Foley for turning me onto these Zig Ziglar sales tapes back in 1996. I drove all over Texas listening to them, and it really turned my sales around. Mark, you know we will always be brothers.

I want to thank Michael Norton for bringing me into so many opportunities along the way. Hiring me to work at Ziglar really turned my life around. God bless you, Michael. I love you man.

I want to thank Zig Ziglar. Your impact on my life was enormous Zig, and I'm so grateful to be able to live in your legacy. I want to keep your principles and teaching current for the next generation of people who need help.

Tom Ziglar, you are a wonderful person and a brother. Thank you for your contributions to the book, for writing my foreword, and more importantly, for being a difference maker. I'm so honored to be a part of the Ziglar family.

Bryan Flanagan, you will always be "Coach" to me. Thank you for teaching me the TRUST sales process and so many more things like presentation skills and strategies for success. You are the best sales trainer, and your corny jokes always kept me laughing.

Kevin Borden, thank you for being my best friend. You taught me everything I know about digital x-ray technology, and I thrived because of the time we spent teaching each other. I love you, dude.

Neil Shillig, thank you for helping with all the real estate transactions and finding houses and renters for me. I could not have done it without your help.

Jen Guidry, you are such a rock star, thank you for getting me all my mortgages and for your contribution to the book. You are a dynamic person with great influence. I can't wait to see what you do next.

Laurie Magers, thank you so much for helping me organize this book. Your advice and eye for detail got me on the right track. God bless you for all the years you have supported Zig and the Ziglar family.

Thank you, Lord, for saving me, for bringing these people into my life when I needed their help so badly. Thank you for helping me change my life and for your grace, mercy, and forgiveness along the way. Jeremiah 29:11

www.ingramcontent.com/pod-product-compliance
Lightning Source LLC
Chambersburg PA
CBHW060159100426
42744CB00007B/1093